.75

D0108049

NO BOX SEATS IN THE KINGDOM

**Sermons For The Sundays
After Pentecost (Last Third)
Cycle B, Gospel Texts**

William G. Carter

CSS Publishing Company, Inc., Lima, Ohio

Copyright © 1996 by
CSS Publishing Company, Inc.
Lima, Ohio

Scripture quotations are from the *New Revised Standard Version of the Bible*, copyright 1989 by the Division of Christian Education of the National Council of the Churches of Christ in the USA. Used by permission.

Library of Congress Cataloging-in-Publication Data

Carter, William G., 1960-
    No box seats in the kingdom : sermons for the Sundays after Pentecost (last third) : cycle B, Gospel texts / William G. Carter.
        p.   cm.
    ISBN 0-7880-0805-6 (pbk. : alk. paper)
    1. Presbyterian Church — United States — Sermons. 2. Sermons, American. 3. Bible. N.T. Gospels — Sermons. 4. Church year sermons. I. Title.
BX9178.C35N6   1996
252'.6—dc20   96-11805
                                                                                CIP

This book is available in the following formats, listed by ISBN:
    0-7880-0805-6   Book
    0-7880-0806-4   IBM 3 1/2
    0-7880-0807-2   Mac
    0-7880-0808-0   Sermon Prep

To the Homiletical Feast,
an astonishing gathering of preachers
who remind me each year of three truths:
scripture is a gift to be shared,
preaching is too important to do alone,
and
life is best lived in the company of friends.

Table Of Contents

C — Revised Common Lectionary; L — Lutheran Lectionary; RC — Roman Catholic Lectionary

Introduction:
After The Water Has Dried

Margaret Rose Carter was baptized on October 1, 1995. It was, for most concerned, a memorable occasion. Her parents were not nervous, having successfully negotiated the baptism of her older sister Kate three years earlier. Meg wore the same ivory satin baptismal gown her sister had worn, a gown cut from their mother's wedding dress. Most of the same family members were present, beaming the same radiant smiles.

Meg's baptism was slightly complicated by the presence of her older sister. Kate fidgeted while the minister spoke the ancient words of scripture. Her father gripped her shoulders as water was splashed on her sister's head. Within seconds of the event, Kate broke free with a delighted squeal and moved quickly to her infant sister. She cupped her hands around the baby's head. "Daddy," she said in a pre-schooler's not-quite-whisper, "Meg's head is wet. She really was baptized!"

Those of us who take the Christian faith seriously want to know that every baptism really happens. In baptism, God claims us through water and the Word. God announces our citizenship in a new dominion before we even know it. God gathers us in a love that precedes all human relationships and family ties. Baptism signifies that we belong to God. So how will we know that a baptism is real? The answer lies in how we respond to God's grace. What matters to God is not whether our brows are still wet from the baptismal font, but *how we shall live after the water has dried.*

Let's face it: we are unfinished disciples and imperfect followers of Jesus. Baptism may be the clearest moment in the church when God's claim on human life is announced. Yet some time must pass before we see whether each baptism will "take."

When the church baptized us, we were adopted into a community of faith that is marked by selfless commitment, generous service, and genuine gratitude. We need to be guided by this community as we grow into our mature membership in God's family, and weaned from the world's selfish actions, stingy habits, and resentful attitudes. Such growth is both painful and rewarding. When we walk the road of discipleship we frequently move three steps forward and two steps back.

These sermons are conversations along the way. At first glance, they are a bag of untidy scraps, a piecemeal collection of sermons from the church's most ordinary time of year. Yet they are stitched together by a call to Christian maturity, as I have heard it through a variety of scripture lessons from the lectionary. In these pages, I do my best to offer a gospel word to those who find themselves troubled by relationships, tainted by affluence, tired of the career ladder, traumatized by persecution, or threatened by death. Every attempt is made to interpret each scripture text within its literary and theological context. The greater aim, however, is to cultivate full-grown disciples of Jesus Christ.

The sermons are also held together because they are words *from* the church *to* the church. Those of us who preach do so only in the presence of a baptized community that is under obligation to "grow up in every way . . . into Christ" (Ephesians 4:15). When we were baptized, we were gathered into a community full of people we would not otherwise choose; yet that is where faith must be lived and worked out. One of my favorite definitions of the church is *a group of baptized people that we are stuck with.* We follow Jesus within the give and take of congregational life. The local congregation is where sermons are spoken and heard and where disciples are commissioned and sent.

I can write these words only because of the communities of faith that surround me with love, honesty, and support. In most cases, the people of First Presbyterian Church of Clarks Summit, Pennsylvania, were the first people to hear these sermons. I composed these words with their faces in my mind and their concerns on my heart. As these sermons appear in print, others will have an opportunity to eavesdrop on conversations between a particular congregation of God's people and their scriptures.

8

Within the church, I am sustained by many circles of encouragement and companionship. Special thanks go to my colleagues on the church staff who do the work of Christ's ministry in all seasons, including the dusty season of a major building renovation that occurred while this book was being put together. They include Nancy Owens, Jamie Urso, Barbara Muntzel, Christine Katsock, Maud Thomas, Joanie Garnecki, and Frank Garnecki. I am humbled by their dedication, love, and skill. What's more, friends like Harry Freebairn and Linda Williams have called me out of the blue to encourage me to keep writing, while friends in a continuing education group called "The Homiletical Feast" have helped me discern what needs to be written.

Most of all, I am grateful to the three bright-eyed females in my household. My wife, Colleen Lane Carter, has offered constant encouragement while I sat at the dining room table, tapping on a laptop computer. She always gives wise counsel when verbs and nouns do not match. When my spirits sag, she suggests pizza.

My daughters Katherine Ann (Kate) and Margaret Rose (Meg) have patiently waited for me to finish this volume. Even now, Kate beckons for me to join her in dancing to the Count Basie Orchestra, while infant Meg coos in search of her voice. Meg will find her voice as certainly as her big sister did before her. As both of them grow, I pray the church will be bold enough to teach them a gospel worth speaking and a resurrection life worth living.

After all, they have been baptized. Their lives matter to the Eternal One. And all heaven waits to see how they, and we, shall speak and live, now that the water has dried.

William G. Carter
Clarks Summit, PA

9

Invitation
To Community

We have a problem today. Here we are, gathered at worship as the household of God. Through baptism we belong to a worldwide community of faith. Each time we gather, we have an opportunity to pray together and recommit ourselves to peace. Now that we are here, we have to deal with a troublesome and potentially divisive text from the Gospel of Mark. Some Pharisees put Jesus to the test by asking him what he thought about divorce. His response, in turn, has always put a peace-loving church to the test.

Jesus' teaching about divorce provokes a variety of responses. Some people hear the text snarl at them like a wild animal. Others grow angry when they simply hear the words, and vow to cross their fingers the next time they encounter that piece of scripture. Still others wish their preacher would stand up and swing this text like a club; family life is spinning out of control, they claim, and the church should push us back to simpler, more Victorian times.

It is no wonder many ministers avoid this text. One year the lectionary appointed it for World Communion Sunday, of all days. A clergy friend said, "I have a congregation full of divorced people. How dare I invite them to the Lord's table with a passage that sounds so fierce?" Another minister, a divorced woman, avoided the issue altogether. She ignored the first ten verses and moved directly ahead to discuss the blessing Jesus offered to little children.

So we have a problem today. Is there any way for all of us to hear something helpful in this text?

Would it help to note this passage of scripture is a "controversy narrative"? It is one of those stories where Jesus was examined by his opponents. His back was up against the wall. Some Pharisees put him to the test. "Tell us how you read the law: Is it legal for a man to divorce his wife? Yes or no?" They wanted Jesus to give his answer. Of course, the Pharisees of that time were divided on the issue among themselves.[1] Maybe Jesus' opponents thought if they could pin him down on the issue, they could criticize whatever answer he gave. Jesus, as we've heard, throws the matter back into their laps and exposes their hypocrisy. If anybody wants to play the judgment game, they themselves will be judged. Those who wield a club will themselves be clubbed. Does it help to tell you that? Maybe, maybe not.

Would it help to remind us that when Jesus spoke about divorce, he was responding against the backdrop of casual attitudes that men held about marriage? In that time and culture, the husband had all the power. If a wife burned the supper or did not bear enough male children, her husband could merely turn his back to her and say three times, "I divorce you." Then he was free to find a more appealing mate. His ex-wife was left standing alone in humiliation. Her only recourse was to return to her father's home in shame and hope he would receive her. So Jesus sought to put some teeth into the marriage covenant. The issue was not discovering a few loopholes in the divorce law. No, Jesus spoke of the promise of creation. Men and women were made as partners for one another, created as gifts for one another. Together we are joint heirs of God's creation. Essentially Jesus was saying, "Husbands, take your wives seriously!" Does it help to tell you that? Maybe, maybe not.

Perhaps it should be said, as Gordon Wenham notes, that within Jesus' pronouncement is a "revolutionary statement that puts wives on an equal basis within marriage."[2] That is, when Jesus says, "Whoever divorces his wife and marries another commits adultery *against her,*" he affirms that women in marriage relationships are equal partners who deserve the same legal rights as men. Then he goes on to add, "*Whoever divorces her husband* and marries another commits adultery against him." How striking a statement for women in ancient Jewish society! Women had no rights. They could not divorce their husbands. But the word of Jesus was spoken for a new day, to a church where women were considered full partners in God's household. In other words, Jesus was also saying, "Wives, take your husbands seriously." Is it helpful to tell you that about this text? Maybe, maybe not.

Maybe it would be helpful to point out the Bible does not have one overriding prohibition on divorce. This may surprise you, but the Bible speaks with many voices on the matter. The promise of creation says we were made for one another, but says nothing about those occasions when relationships are ripped asunder (Genesis 2:24). Is it lawful for couples to divorce? Moses assumed it was lawful, but for him it was the husband's prerogative (Deuteronomy 24:1-4). The prophet Malachi claimed God hates divorce, equating it with an act of violence (Malachi 2:16). But Ezra the priest lamented how the men of Israel had married women of other races and foreign beliefs. "Get rid of them," he said to the men. "Send them away!" (Ezra 10:10-11).

When we get to the New Testament, Jesus gives his unique word, "Whatever God has brought together, let no one separate." That causes some to wonder if God really *does* bring every couple together. Some relationships probably began on more primitive urges. Then the apostle Paul, who wasn't married, gave a surprising amount of advice from a distance. One thing he said was, "If you are unequally yoked, keep the marriage together for the sake of the children; but if it does not work, then divorce is one choice among a lot of difficult choices" (1 Corinthians 7:12-15).

The Bible addresses a variety of situations when the promise of creation is disrupted or ripped apart. The question is: What does God intend for us? What is God's promise for creation?

Does God want everybody to be married? No, that's ridiculous. As the unmarried apostle Paul said, some single people should stay as they are (1 Corinthians 7:8-9). Singleness is their gift. No one needs to be married to belong to God. That's why whenever a faithful church puts out a membership directory, it lists women by their first names, by their *baptized* names. God gathers the church at the baptismal font, not at the marriage altar.

So what does God want for us? More than anything else, God wants people to live in peace as a community. Beneath the crusted corals of various interpretations, that's where this text points us. God wants us to recognize other people as partners, not strangers; to live as companions, not competitors. Jesus was doing something more than confronting the reality of divorce. He was attacking a human trait that disrupts the life of a community. He called it "hardness of heart," a deadly condition of the soul when compassion freezes, when care collapses, when love turns to stone.

This hardness of heart makes single people feel like they are not welcome in a congregation full of couples. One church, for instance, announced the formation of a new fellowship group in their worship bulletin. The group called itself, "Spares and Pairs." The pastor, who was a young widower, called the well-intentioned (and mostly married) founders of the group together. "For God's sake," he fumed, "what makes anybody think a single person would want to be called a 'spare'?"

The church is called to welcome single people, whether they are newly single or have always been so. God calls the church to welcome anybody whom God sends, without preference or prejudice. Hospitality is a fundamental virtue of the faithful. The church announces to single people, "You are welcome here, as you are."

Let's also recognize the hardness of heart which makes divorced people feel excluded from the promises of God. No person ever gets married with the intention of getting divorced. Every couple who marries does so with the intent "to have and to hold, from this day forward." That is the promise. Yet sometimes the promise can no longer be kept. Relationships break down. People break down. Should that happen, the church is called once again to offer hospitality. We say, "Come and join us, especially if you are broken, and we will tell you about the Christ who binds our wounds and holds us together." If you are divorced, you need to hear the church say, loudly and clearly, that you are also welcome here, as you are, with whatever you bring.

What's more, let's acknowledge in our midst the hardness of heart which endangers a lot of our marriages. Many myths exist about divorce. One myth is that fifty percent of all marriages in this country end in divorce. It simply is not true. The actual percentage is much lower. The myth began about twenty years ago when an amateur statistician, probably a preacher, noticed the number of divorces in a given year equaled half the number of weddings in that same year. He concluded fifty percent of all marriages will fall apart. The statistics are skewed. As any divorced person will tell you, there are many more married people than divorced people. That is one reason why so many divorced people feel so alone.

The fact such myths continue is evidence of how difficult it is to be married these days. We live in a fast-paced society that undermines our ability to know one another deeply and intimately. Our culture worships self-fulfillment over patience, mercy, and steadfast love. It's difficult to keep a long-term commitment when popular books push instant gratification and self-help. It is not easy to pledge your troth to anybody in a "me-first" society.

God wants us to live in peace with one another. Therefore the church is called to support and strengthen marriages, for a marriage is the smallest form of community. As the Presbyterian wedding service announces, "God gave us marriage for the well-being of human society." We cannot expect peace in our world unless we claim some sense of peace in our households.

Working for such peace may require us to stand up against some prevailing thoughts in our culture. Wendell Berry is a Kentucky farmer and a champion of community health. He also writes award-winning articles and stories. A few years ago, he wrote a brief article for *Harper's Magazine* where he explained why he was never going to buy a computer. First, he already had a good typewriter. Second, his wife Tanya helps him with the proofreading and production of his work.

Berry anticipated a negative response about his use of a typewriter. Our age honors bigger and faster machines with a certain kind of technological fundamentalism. What surprised him, however, were the many antagonistic letters he received about the nature of his marriage. Angry people wrote, "How dare you think of your wife that way! It's positively Neanderthal. She is an individual, separate and distinct, with her own life to live."

15

Berry mused over what could be wrong with the notion of sharing daily tasks with one's spouse. As he observed, a lot of couples live separate lives, detached and cut off from one another. They pretend to be married, but they divide things up as if they are divorced. He went on to note,

> *There are, however, still married couples who understand themselves as belonging to their marriage, to each other, and to their children. What they have they have in common, and so, to them, helping each other does not seem merely to damage their ability to compete against each other. To them, "mine" is not so powerful or necessary a pronoun as "ours."*[3]

What does it mean to live like a community —— in our homes, in our church, and in our world? That's a good question to ask a church that gathers around the Lord's table. No matter how alienated we feel elsewhere, God welcomes every person here. Regardless of how broken we may be, God's table is the banquet of mercy. We do not deserve the invitation, if only for our hardness of heart, yet we are gathered by a grace that covers us all. And when we leave, we are under obligation to extend the hospitality of God to all people, as they are, wherever they are.

So let us learn from a gracious God whose love embraces every one of us. Gathered by God's hospitality, we can discover how to live together and love one another, through Jesus Christ, our Lord.

———————————

1. John R. Donahue, "Mark," *Harper's Bible Commentary*, 1988 ed., p. 996.

2. Gordon J. Wenham, "Divorce," *The Oxford Companion to the Bible* (New York: Oxford University Press, 1993), p. 170.

3. Wendell Berry, "Feminism, the Body, and the Machine," *What Are People For?* (San Francisco: North Point Press, 1990), pp. 180-1.

Love
And Money

A seminary professor named Stanley Hauerwas has a novel idea about how churches should receive new members. A teacher of Christian ethics at Duke University, he has written about the church's need for honesty and has called us to tell the truth as a "community of character."

To this end, he has a modest proposal. Whenever people join the church, Hauerwas thinks they should stand and answer four questions:

• Who is your Lord and Savior? The response: "Jesus Christ."
• Do you trust in him and seek to be his disciple? "I do."
• Will you be a faithful member of this congregation? The answer: "I will."
• Finally, one last question: *What is your annual income?*[1]

You heard me correctly. When people join the church, Dr. Hauerwas thinks they ought to name their Lord and Savior and tell fellow church members how much money they make.

It is obvious Hauerwas does not serve as a pastor of a congregation. His idea just wouldn't work, especially in the American church. Most church members believe salary figures are more sacred than prayer, and would quickly tell an inquisitive minister to snoop around somewhere else. What's more, parish experience tempers the questions a minister asks of church members. Most pastors quickly learn how to dance around the issue of money without ever naming it.

A young minister went out to serve his first congregation. Early one November, he told the sexton to go out to the bulletin board on the street corner and put up the words, "Stewardship Sunday." He put together a stewardship sermon and preached it to the congregation. Afterwards someone came up and said, "Pastor, thank you for that sermon. When I saw the bulletin board, I was a little anxious. But your sermon calmed my fears."

The minister said, "I'm glad to hear it. Did I say something helpful?"

"Oh, Reverend, it was better than that," the man said. "Today you said absolutely nothing at all."

It is tempting to keep silent in the church when it comes to money. We dance around the issue with large, general steps. The church talks in generalities about the electric bill, the rising cost of church school curricula, and mission projects worthy of our support. Those are worthy topics of conversation. That's usually where the conversation remains — with the list of the good services the church provides. Any actual mention of money seems distasteful.

A few years ago, an interchange of letters appeared in a nationally syndicated newspaper column.

> *Dear Abby: We are not overly religious people, but we do like to go to church once in a while. It seems to me that every time we turn around, we are hit for money. I thought religion was free. I realize that churches have to have some money, but I think it is getting to be a racket. Just what do churches do with all their money? Curious in North Jersey.*

Abby wrote back,

> *Dear Curious: Even priests, ministers and rabbis must eat. Since they work full-time at their tasks, their churches must support them. Staff ... and musicians must also be paid. Buildings must be maintained, heated, lighted and beautified ... Custodial staff must eat and feed their*

families. Most churches engage in philanthropic work (aid to the needy, missions, and education); hence, they have their financial obligations. Even orchids, contrary to folklore, do not live on air. Churches can't live on air either. Religions, like water, may be free, but when they pipe it to you, you've got to help pay for the piping. And the piper.[2]

A lot of stewardship committees probably cheered when they read those words in the newspaper. It's good to hear Abby spell out the expenditures of a typical church budget. Yet she is shortsighted in two ways. First, when we give our money to the church, we are doing more than supporting an institution; we are participating in the work God is doing within these walls. The utility bills, the salaries, the insurance premiums, and the church school supplies are all means to a far greater end. The Holy Spirit has descended upon this church, upon this people, and I, for one, want to support what God is doing through people like you and me.

The second problem is the assumption that religion is "free." The Christian faith is a costly faith. It demands a radical commitment to Jesus Christ. Those who would follow Jesus must pick up their crosses and give their lives as he has given his life for us. Anything less is discounted grace.

That brings us to the heart of the gospel text from the tenth chapter of Mark. It begins as a success story. Jesus is preaching about the kingdom of God, traveling here and there. Somebody runs up, kneels down, and says, "Jesus, what must I do to get whatever you've been talking about? What must I do to claim the life of God's eternal realm?"

Obviously that's the kind of question Jesus wants to hear. For seven chapters he has been surrounded by disciples who chase away children, quiver in disbelief, and argue over which of them is the greatest. Finally, here's an honest seeker who wants to know what it takes. What must he do? His conversation with Jesus discusses the ethical demands of the law: don't murder, don't lie, don't steal, and take care of your parents. Do these things and live.

19

The anonymous man said, "I've kept all of those things." He had become a successful seeker.

So the story becomes a love story. Mark says Jesus "loved" this man. In the Gospel of Mark, there's no other place where it says Jesus loved anybody. Usually the Lord is too busy, going immediately here and immediately there. He heals one sick person after another. He shouts at wind storms and screams at demons. He never slows down to love anybody, especially his disciples. In Mark's book, the twelve disciples appear as blockheads who stood around and scratched their heads whenever Jesus said or did anything significant. Mark never says Jesus loved Peter, James, John, or the others. But he insists Jesus loved this man. Maybe that's because (a) the man sought the kingdom of God and (b) he did what God commanded.

But something was wrong. Not only is this the only occasion where Mark says Jesus loved somebody. This is the only time in Mark's gospel when Jesus invited someone to follow him and the person could not do it. The reason for the refusal is given: "He went away grieving, for he had many possessions" (Mark 10:22).

Maybe Stanley Hauerwas is right. Perhaps we can't truly join the ranks of those who follow Jesus until we can come clean about the role of money in our lives. Money can become an organizing center of our lives, a human-made deity that competes with the God of Abraham and Sarah. As someone notes, "Money has no material force except as people attribute force to it. Money as an object is not the master of states, of armies, of the masses, or of the mind except by humanity's consent to its authority. Money would be absolutely nothing, materially speaking, without human consent."[3] The bad news in our gospel story is there are occasions when the desire for money — for having it, holding it, keeping it — becomes more important than anything else.

D.H. Lawrence tells a story about a family with a boy and two little girls. They lived in a nice house with a garden. Yet the family felt an anxiety: there was never enough money. Both mother and father had small incomes, but they didn't have enough to reach the social position they desired. The father pursued business leads that never materialized. The mother tried to earn more money, but her failures etched deep lines into her face.

In time, their home became haunted with the unspoken phrase, "There must be more money." No one ever said it aloud, least of all the children. But the words filled the home, especially when expensive toys filled the nursery.

> *Behind the shining modern rocking-horse, behind the smart doll's house, a voice would start whispering: "There **must** be more money. There **must** be more money." The children could hear it all the time, though nobody said it aloud. And the children would stop playing, to listen, for a moment. They would look into each other's eyes, to see if they had all heard. And each one saw in the eyes of the other two that they too had heard. "There **must** be more money. There **must** be more money." Yet nobody ever said it aloud. The whisper was everywhere, and therefore no one spoke it. Just as no one ever says, "We are breathing," in spite of the fact that breath is coming and going all the time.*[4]

That haunting whisper can be heard in a lot of homes. A quiet voice says, "There must be more money," even though money is coming and going all the time. Two kinds of people want more money — those who don't have it and those who do. Either way, the gospel calls our priorities into question.

Jesus loved a rich man as he loved nobody else. When he invited him to follow as a disciple, the man turned and walked away. Jesus said, "You lack something." What was he talking about? The man had money. Mark doesn't say how much, but we can assume he had a lot of things that others enjoy. He had a nice house with a sturdy roof over his head. He had somebody to dust the furniture and someone to mow the lawn. He put food on the table every night, and nobody in his home ever wanted for anything. He could afford attractive clothes for his family. He paid his mortgage on time. He always covered the monthly minimum on his credit cards, with room to spare some. He had everything money could buy. But the one thing he lacked was *freedom*.

Jesus did not command the man to become destitute, nor to take on the burden of voluntary poverty. Neither did he compel him to empty his pockets. Rather he summoned the man to cut all ties to the things of the world which enslave and tangle. He invited the man to become free:

• free from having to possess things;
• free from determining his importance by the size of his bank account;
• free from the invisible entanglements of wealth;
• free from the quiet, deadly grip of materialism.

What does it mean to become free in this way? Ask a family who dumped some possessions at a recent garage sale. After discovering how much junk they had accumulated over the last few years, they put an ad in the newspaper and announced a garage sale. The dust cleared by noon on Saturday. The family made a bit of money, which allowed them to buy some more junk. Now they have a house full of new junk, which is better than old junk. Of course, they can't yet tell the difference.

To sum up, the gospel lesson proclaims good news and bad news this morning. The good news is nobody who clings to his riches can get into the kingdom of God. Or is that bad news? The good news is anything is possible with God; God can purge us of all our possessiveness. Or is that bad news? Each of us must decide.

One thing is for sure. If we want to follow Jesus, we had better brace ourselves. He calls us to serve a God who loves us, a God who will keep disturbing us until we finally relinquish our grip on money and possessions. Once we say yes to God, we can expect holy disruptions in our lives until the day when God alone shall purge and possess our hearts.

---

1. Stanley Hauerwas, Center for Continuing Education, Princeton Theological Seminary, Princeton, NJ, 1 May 1992.

2. Abigail Van Buren, "Religions need money too, for heaven's sake," *The Scranton Tribune* 30 March 1994: C-2.

3. Jacques Ellul, *Money and Power* (Downers Grove: Intervarsity Press, 1984), p. 81.

4. As quoted in Elizabeth O Connor, *Letters to Scattered Pilgrims* (San Francisco: Harper and Row, Publishers, 1979), pp. 17-18.

No Box Seats
In The Kingdom

Historically speaking, the church has usually painted a pretty picture of the twelve original disciples of Jesus. All except Judas have been considered saints. Pious people have named churches after them, often referring to the first disciples as the rocks upon which Christ has built his church. Yet anybody who hears the Gospel of Mark's stories about the disciples gets a different picture of who they were and what they wanted. Sure, the disciples walked the road with Jesus. They listened as he taught. They watched as he did signs and wonders. They followed where he led. However, according to Mark, they never really got the point. In fact, they frequently looked foolish.

Today we hear about James and John scurrying up to Jesus while the others weren't looking. "Teacher," they said, "we want you to do whatever we ask." That alone is a shameless request. They really didn't have the right to ask for a blank check. Jesus, in his eternal patience, decided to sound them out. "What do you want?" he said. They replied, "On the day when you enter your glory, when you ascend to the throne as King of kings and Lord of lords, we want to sit at your right and at your left."

Well, it was a ridiculous request . . . and when the other ten disciples heard about it, they got angry with James and John. They were upset, not because they thought it was the wrong thing to ask

23

for, but because James and John asked for it *first*. Those two lowly fishermen wanted two box seats in the Kingdom of God, two chairs of honor for that day when Jesus will finally shine in the fullness of his glory.

Today we catch a glimpse of those disciples, looking like children who play "King of the Hill." They shamelessly tried to scramble to the top of the heap. We hear them beg for power, and shake our heads in disbelief.

Perhaps it shocks us to see such blatant self-promotion within the ranks of Christ's disciples. Outside the church, these attitudes are present every day. The world out there encourages us to take the initiative, climb the ladder, and push to the front of the line. "Blessed are the aggressive," says our culture, "for they will get what they want." If that means pulling the boss aside and making a private pitch, then that is what must be done. Like it or not, this is how the world works. Here in the church, it disturbs us to see the same attitudes, even if they may not be immediately obvious.

A Methodist pastor once wrote about power and politics in his denomination. Methodist preachers, he notes, are under the care of a bishop. Bishops, in turn, are Methodist preachers who are elected by fellow Methodist preachers after an extensive campaign for the office in which the candidate tries not to be caught campaigning. As he observes,

> *It is a long-standing Methodist tradition that bishops must not appear to have sought their office and, once elected, the new bishop must make a public declaration that "I didn't seek this office and I didn't want it but, once the Lord calls" … Methodist preachers take all of this with a grain of salt, the same way Baptist congregations have learned to be somewhat skeptical when one of their preachers moves on to a better church claiming, "I hate to leave this church and I would rather stay here, but the Lord calls." Baptists note that the Lord rarely calls someone out of one church into another church unless that church has a higher salary. Methodists have likewise noted that there have been few preachers who, once they are elected bishop, turn the job down.*[1]

24

"Teacher, we want you to put us on your right and on your left. But keep it quiet. Don't make it too obvious. Others may become offended that we asked first." By telling us this story, Mark knows what you and I know: we are prone to the same desire for privilege and protected status. We want a Jesus who will give us what we want, a Lord who can shower a little power on us, a Savior who can make us better than we are.

A number of years ago, a small book appeared for ministers. Titled *The Penguin Principles,* it attempted to help naive clergy get a handle on the people of their congregations. Most of the material in the book was written with tongue in cheek, so it has some truth in it. According to the book, the first principle of church life goes like this: "Despite the pious things we say, at any given time, less than five percent of any group in the church is operating with purely Christian motivation. The other 95 percent is asking, 'What's in it for me?' "[2]

When I first read those words I thought, "Oh, no. That's not true. Church people are inherently generous and gracious. They are always eager to help, remaining free from selfish motives and concerns about getting their own way." Then I tried to gather a youth group from a list of Senior Highs, and one after another said, "What's in it for me?" Somewhat discouraged, I attempted to gather some adults to help me share the work as a youth group advisor. Each one said, "What will I get out of it?"

"Teacher, give us what we want." In one sense Jesus is wrong when he replies, "You don't know what you're asking." We know perfectly well what we are asking. We want God to meet our unlimited needs and help us get ahead.

Yet in a deeper sense, any request for cheap success reveals we do not know what kind of God we meet in Jesus. "Look," he said to his disciples, "we are going up to Jerusalem. And it's uphill all the way. The road is hard and difficult. We face painful twists and turns. There will be suffering, humiliation, and death. There is no easy road to glory. Are you able to drink this cup? Are you able to bear this kind of baptism?"

James and John reply, "Sure, no problem." But do they really know? Do we know?

Jesus came to proclaim the kingdom, the mysterious reign of God that grows like a secret seed, ever so gently, ever so silently, until it becomes the greatest of all plants. One morning, God willing, we will wake up and see this gift of God and we will wonder how it happened. We won't know. The kingdom grows in spite of us, in ways we cannot comprehend.

The key is Jesus himself, who comes with a kind of paradoxical, left-handed power. Recall what Jesus does in the Gospel of Mark. One minute, he screams away the demonic forces that torment human minds, telling them to hush. The next minute, he gathers little children and lepers into the embrace of God. One day he shouts at wind and waves and all the turbulent powers of an unruly creation. Another day he rides a humble donkey into a hostile city. Once Jesus put his fingers in the ears of someone who has never heard the good news of God. Immediately he uses his words as a scalpel for cutting away the cancerous lies that keep people from the health which God intends. In every way, Jesus Christ has come to make a difference in this painful, haunted world. He has come to serve, not to sit on a throne with dull-minded disciples on his right and his left. He has come to give his life to pay off our ransom to the powers and principalities, to set people free from all that can damage, hurt, and destroy.

Are you able to drink that cup? Are you able to share his baptism? Anybody who would follow Jesus must be a servant as he is a servant. It requires a total change in how we live. If we want to follow Jesus, we can't live for ourselves anymore. We must give our lives in service to others.

Richard Foster tells about receiving a phone call from a friend. The friend's wife had taken the car, and he wanted to know if Richard could take him on a number of errands. Richard was preparing to teach a college class, but since the man was his friend he reluctantly agreed. As he ran out the door, car keys in hand, he grabbed a book to read along the way. It was a book by Dietrich Bonhoeffer called *Life Together*.

Foster picked up his friend, and the errands did not go well. There were plenty of stops and starts, traffic was bad, and precious time kept ticking away. Finally they pulled into a parking lot, the friend got out, and Richard stayed behind with his book. He opened it to the bookmark, and read these words:

> *The second service that one should perform for another in a Christian community is that of active helpfulness. This means, initially, simple assistance in trifling, external matters. There is a multitude of these things wherever people live together. Nobody is too good for the meanest service. One who worries about the loss of time that such petty, outward acts of helpfulness entail is usually taking the importance of his own career too solemnly.*[3]

Are you able to drink that cup? Are you able to share his baptism? If we want to follow Jesus, we must change some of the ways our culture does business. We live with a kind of institutional selfishness, where many industries stop at nothing to make a buck, regardless of how the common good is affected. We have more fast food restaurants than factories, more catalogs than cattle, more microchips than meaning. We live in a service economy. Ironically, there is little service in ways that really count. As sociologist Robert Bellah notes, a lot of companies couldn't care less about making the world a better place. If they have any kind of social responsibility, it is "a kind of public relations whipped cream decorating the corporate pudding."[4]

What if church people who work for our great corporations decided to speak up? What if we served the world by advocating the things we really need: like an equitable wage for anybody who can work, an environment that nurtures human health, a means for strangers to live in peace, and, most of all, a sense of holy purpose whereby our daily work counts for something?

Are you able to drink that cup? Are you able to share his baptism? I don't know. I do know if we want to follow Jesus, we must rethink what it means to be the church, especially in a culture that worships success. The kind of church God wants is not a church that bows down before stature, power, or worldly achievement. No, it's the kind of church that sets people free to serve God, every day, in the places where God sends them. We need a church that produces people who are servants just like Jesus.

A few years ago, Joel Gregory became the pastor of First Baptist Church of Dallas, an impressive congregation with almost thirty thousand members. It was the crowning achievement of his career. First Baptist Church occupies five city blocks in downtown Dallas. It houses two schools, a college, and a radio station. The church gave him a nice home, memberships in exclusive country clubs, and luxury box seats for Dallas Cowboys football games. They weren't box seats for the kingdom, but in Dallas a box seat for one is as good as a box seat for another.

But something went wrong in Gregory's pastorate. Church leaders wanted more members; thirty thousand weren't enough. People wanted the physical plant to grow; five city blocks wasn't big enough. Most of all, everyone expected Gregory to tag along behind his predecessor, W. A. Criswell, who had served that congregation for 46 years and who, despite his announcements to the contrary, showed no signs of retiring. "There wasn't room for both of us," Joel Gregory said. "The whole zoo of human ambition and power and ego is the fabric of some superchurches." A power struggle began, dividing the church into opposing sides. One day in September 1992, Gregory stunned many Southern Baptists by resigning from that prominent pulpit.

Today he travels through Fort Worth neighborhoods as a door-to-door salesman. A lot of people say he's a failure. Joel Gregory says otherwise. "For the first time in my life, at 46, I'm learning what it means to be a servant," he says. "It gives me a different view of Christ, and a different view of the real needs of human beings."[5]

Jesus said, "Are you able to drink my cup? Are you able to share my baptism? Are you able to walk with me, giving yourself to others in a life of service?" If we dare say yes, we must remember the road of discipleship is uphill all the way, and it leads to the foot of the cross. Whoever would follow Jesus must follow him there. He never promised anything else.

———————

1. William H. Willimon, *And the Laugh Shall Be First* (Nashville: Abingdon Press, 1986), p. 94.

2. David S. Belasic and Paul M. Schmidt, *The Penguin Principles* (Lima, Ohio: CSS Publishing, Inc., 1986), p. 17.

3. Richard Foster, *Celebration of Discipline* (San Francisco: Harper and Row, 1978), pp. 117-8.

4. Robert Bellah, et. al., *Habits of the Heart* (Los Angeles: University of California Press, 1985), p. 290.

5. David Briggs, "Ex-superchurch pastor now sells cemetery plots," *Scranton Times* 2 October 1994.

Can You See
Where We're Going?

A cigar-chomping realtor was driving around a young couple to search for their first dream house. After listening to their concerns about mortgage points, maintenance costs, and school systems, he decided to give them a bit of advice. "I've been selling homes for 23 years," he said, "and I've discovered only three things matter when you're buying a home: location, location, location."

To prove his point, he drove the couple to see two homes. The paint was peeling on the first house, and the driveway was heaving in spots. "It may be a handyman's special," he said, "but look at the view." The house sat at the foot of a purple mountain, adjacent to ten acres of untouched forest. Then the group went to see a charming two-story stone farmhouse with five bedrooms, a big kitchen, and plenty of closets. "Everything's immaculate," the wife exclaimed after a brief tour inside. "In fact, we might buy it if it was located somewhere else." Then she pulled back a curtain to see an interstate highway and a busy airport runway.

Location, location, location. It is a good rule in considering real estate. It is also a good rule in biblical interpretation. Anybody who wants to know the deeper meaning of a biblical text can benefit by looking around its neighborhood.

At first glance, the story of Jesus and Bartimaeus looks like a typical healing story. A sightless beggar alongside the road regains

31

his vision at the word of Jesus. The deed fulfills the promise of the prophet Isaiah, "The eyes of the blind shall be opened" (Isaiah 35:5). The fact that the blind man is named is somewhat unusual, but easily explained. When Matthew and Luke tell the story, the beggar is anonymous. In Mark, he is the son of Timaeus, literally "Bar-Timaeus." Perhaps Mark's community knew him, and the writer tells us his story as if to say, "You know old Bart, who sits in the fourth pew by the window? Here's the story of how he began to see."

Yet look where this story is told: immediately before Jesus enters Jerusalem to give his life on the cross. This is the last time Jesus heals anybody in the Gospel of Mark. It may be the only occasion when the healing turns out as Jesus wished. Other healings by Jesus prompted misinterpretation[1], disobedience[2], and hard-hearted opposition.[3] Those around the fringes of each healing were inclined to superficial hero-worship or fear.[4] Yet Bartimaeus followed Jesus "on the way," that is, down the road to Jerusalem. Jesus' healing ministry was completed in a man who was a beggar but now became his disciple.

What's more, this is the second occasion in the Gospel of Mark where Jesus healed someone who could not see. In chapter eight, a man at Bethsaida needed extra help in having his sight restored. Jesus touched him once and asked what he could see. "I see people," was the response, "but they look like walking trees" (Mark 8:24). So Jesus placed his hands on the man's eyes for a second time. Then the man could see. By contrast, the healing of Bartimaeus went much smoother. Mark says the blind beggar leapt up and came stumbling across the road. Like other beggars, his cloak was both his blanket and his means for panhandling. The cloak was always spread out before him to gather coins tossed to him in pity. When Jesus drew near, Bartimaeus threw off the cloak and sprang up, ready to be healed. He gave up the old life of begging and prepared himself for the new life of health.

But most striking is what happens between the first healing of the blind person in chapter eight and the second healing of blind Bartimaeus in chapter ten. Throughout this section of Mark's Gospel, the disciples of Jesus do not see a thing. Typical of their spiritual blindness is the conversation that occurs immediately before our text. Jesus asked James and John, "What do you want me to do for you?" Ignoring his repeated predictions of the cross, they said, "Grant us to sit at your right hand and your left, in your glory" (Mark 10:37). Then Jesus asked Bartimaeus the same question, "What do you want me to do for you?" He replied, "Let me see again."

In all of scripture, there is no greater distinction between people than what lies behind those two answers. Jesus comes with the power of the kingdom and says, "What can I do for you?" One response is to ask the Lord to help us get ahead, to seat us in a prestigious place, to move us to a better address. As appealing as that is, it is one request Jesus cannot grant. "It's not my business," he said. "The Son of Man came not to be served, but to serve, and to give his life a ransom for many" (Mark 10:45). But Bartimaeus said, "Let me see again." That is one task Jesus can perform; he can make it possible for people to see. The question is whether or not we really want to have our eyes opened.

In my denomination, there is a weekly magazine full of church news, editorial commentary, and Bible study hints. It also advertises some job openings for ministers who want to relocate to a new church. Knowing a few congregations that are seeking new ministers, I imagined two different advertisements. The first said:

> *We're a large congregation with a lot to offer. Our beautiful sanctuary has Tiffany windows which inspire us to worship God. A large endowment enables us to maintain a full program. Our commitment to the elderly recently prompted us to install a new elevator. Many of our members are influential in our city; they include business leaders, professional people, and a former state governor. Our last pastor was a published poet, and we are looking for another polished preacher to inspire us to high ideals and move us to laughter and tears. Salary and benefits package are generous, and negotiable for the right candidate.*

On the other hand, I imagined a second advertisement that said something like this:

> *We are an aging congregation in a troubled city. There have been recent shootings in our neighborhood, probably drug-related. For the past decade, our church has served as a reconciling force in our city. We minister to the poor, the illiterate, and the aging, as well as to a group home across the street. One of our greatest needs is to bridge the gap between affluent members who commute to worship and the neighborhood where our building is located. Our last pastor was instrumental in beginning a chapter of Habitat for Humanity, and we desire a new minister with similar energy, imagination, and interest in urban ministry. People of courage are invited to apply.*

Would it surprise you to learn that those are two potential advertisements for the same church? Both advertisements are true of one congregation I know. The difference between the ads lies in *what they claim to see.* Is the church of Jesus called to sit at the high places in stained glass glory? Or is it our business to stay on the road to the cross?

The truth is people see only what they want to see. The Gospel of Mark provides plenty of evidence to substantiate this truth. For all of Jesus' incredible deeds in that book, his own disciples never see that he has come as one who serves. Jesus makes the deaf to hear, the speechless to sing, and the lame to dance. But the vision of the twelve disciples is clouded by expectations of their own advancement and assumptions about their own success. They do not see Jerusalem right down the road.

The crowds surrounding Jesus also did not see where he was headed. When Bartimaeus heard Jesus was coming, he cried out, "Son of David, have mercy on me." The crowd insisted, "Bartimaeus, be quiet," because the phrase "Son of David" could put Jesus in danger. It was the people's way to refer to the Messiah. If the beggar kept shouting for the Son of David, Roman legions would take notice. Religious officials would raise their eyebrows in curiosity. Zealots would sharpen their swords. The poor and downtrodden would brighten in anticipation. No wonder many "sternly ordered him to be quiet." They saw no reason to prematurely kindle a revolution.

The irony is that, even in his blindness, Bartimaeus clearly saw Jesus as the Messiah, the promised Son of David, the One who came to turn the world upside down. "What do you want me to do for you?" Jesus asked. "Give me eyes to see," said the beggar.

As Ched Myers notes, faith according to the Gospel of Mark is "the determination to shed denial and face the world as it is, in order to struggle for what could be. Remaining clear-eyed is a constant struggle."[5] The world can distort our vision. Like people who have been wearing the same pair of eyeglasses for the past 25 years, we may have gone out of focus and not even known it. We begin to enjoy our own importance, or we protect ourselves from criticism, or we start believing we have seen it all. Whatever the case, our vision for life can grow accustomed to all kinds of distortions. Maybe we compromise ideals we once held dearly. Or we defend our tired opinions from any act of God. Or one day we wake up to discover we have become content to live without any dreams.

And so the good news comes in the request, "Teacher, let me see again." In effect Bartimaeus said, "Lord, let me toss aside all my vain attempts for security and status, and follow you, come what may." That's what it means to see through the eyes of faith. When Bartimaeus regained his sight, when he was free to go wherever his eyes led him, he chose to follow Jesus on his journey to Jerusalem. Of all the places Bartimaeus could have gone, he chose to follow Jesus to the cross.

There's a woman who received eyes to see. A few years ago, with the help of Presbyterian mission money, she helped to establish a halfway house for women who are recovering drug addicts. She schedules twelve-step groups, arranges for child care, and generally tries to get the women back on their feet. In a lot of ways, you would never expect her to be involved with such work. She is even-tempered, gentle, and articulate. But something happened a few years ago that caused her to see anew.

She was a graduate school student in Pittsburgh, looking for a part-time job. A newspaper listed an administrative position with a soup kitchen. That looked interesting, so she clipped it and prepared for the interview. On the day of her interview, she put on a dark blue business suit, put together a manila folder full of resumes and references, and clipped back her hair.

Arriving a few minutes before noon, she saw the sign: "East End Cooperative Ministry." She knocked on the door. Someone inside said, "It's unlocked." She went in, only to find a long line of people in front of her. Disappointment washed over her. Then she realized it was lunch time. The people in the line weren't there for the same interview, they were waiting for soup.

She grew nervous as she looked at the people in line. Some of them, in turn, looked at her. She felt self-conscious about the way she was dressed. Apparently others began to sense her anxiety. A woman in a moth-eaten sweater smiled and tried to make conversation. "Is this your first time here?"

"Yes, it is."

"Don't worry," said the lady in the sweater, "it gets easier."

"The scales fell from my eyes that day," reflected the young woman. "I went there looking for a job, and that woman thought I was there for soup. As far as she knew, the world had been as cruel to me as it was to her. But in the kindest way she could, she welcomed me as a fellow human being. She saw me as someone equally in need, which I was and still am. I didn't realize it at the time, but that was the day when God began to convert me." Looking around the halfway house, she smiled and said, "You see all of these wonderful things God is doing here? They began when God gave us eyes to see where Jesus was leading us."

"What do you want?" asked Jesus. A church could ask for more prestige, a greater impact, and a sense of power. But for a church with the eyes of faith, the answer is clear: "to see thee more clearly, love thee more dearly, follow thee more nearly"[6]...all the way to the cross.

---

1. In Mark 1:21-28, a synogogue crowd misinterprets the healing of a demoniac as a "new teaching" by the preacher Jesus.

2. At least twice, in Mark 1:44-45 and 7:36-37, a healed person disobeys Jesus' request to keep quiet about the miracle.

3. Jesus healed a person with a withered arm on the "wrong" day of the week, and *immediately* his opponents conspired against him (Mark 3:1-6).

4. For instance, see Mark 2:12 and 5:15.

5. Ched Myers, *Who Will Roll Away the Stone?* (Maryknoll, NY: Orbis Books, 1994), p. 46.

6. Stephen Schwartz, "Day by Day," Valando Music Inc. and New Cadenza Music Corporation, 1971.

What To Say When
You Roll Out Of Bed

A few years ago, a radio station ran a contest. Disc jockeys invited their listeners to tune in their clock radios. "Just for fun," they said, "when you wake up to the sound of FM-106, call and tell us the first words you spoke when you rolled out of bed. If you're the third caller, you'll win $106."

It didn't take long for the contest to grow in enthusiasm. The first morning, a buoyant disc jockey said, "Caller number three, what did you say when you rolled out of bed this morning?" A groggy voice said, "Do I smell coffee burning?" Another day, a sleepy clerical worker said, "Oh no, I'm late for work." Somebody else said her first words were, "Honey, did I put out the dog last night?" A muffled curse was immediately heard in the background, and then a man was heard to say, "No, you didn't." It was a funny contest and drew a considerable audience.

One morning, however, the third caller said something unusual. The station phone rang. "Good morning, this is FM-106. You're on the air. What did you say when you rolled out of bed this morning?"

A voice with a Bronx accent replied, "You want to know my first words in the morning?"

The bubbly DJ said, "Yes, sir! Tell us what you said."

The Bronx voice responded, "*Shema*, Israel . . . Hear O Israel, the Lord our God, the Lord is one. And you shall love the Lord your God with all your heart, with all your soul, and with all your might." There was a moment of embarrassed silence. Then the radio announcer said, "Sorry, wrong number," and cut to a commercial.

Try to remember. What did you say when you rolled out of bed today? Chances are, those words set the tone for the rest of the day. For the pious Jew the first words of each morning are always the same, and they were the words spoken that morning on FM-106. They were first spoken by Moses, who said, "Keep these words that I am commanding you today in your heart. Teach them to your children and talk about them when you lie down and when you rise" (Deuteronomy 6:6-7).

In the passage we heard a few minutes ago, some scribe asked Jesus, "Which commandment comes first?" It was probably intended as a trick question. If Jesus picked only one of the 613 commandments, he left himself open for a barrage of criticism from those who favored another commandment. In the Gospel of Mark, there are over a dozen occasions when the scribes oppose Jesus. They mock him, dispute him, and conspire against him. Certainly they will pounce on whatever answer he offers. Yet the scribe immediately backs off when Jesus answers, "You shall love the Lord your God with all your heart."

It is no wonder. The primary obligation for every good Jew has always been to love God with the heart, with the center of all passion and trust. That is the primary purpose of human life. When we were baptized in the name of the Jewish Jesus and adopted into the promises of Israel, we were given the same script to follow. These words name our primary allegiance and bind us to our greatest responsibility: "You shall love the Lord your God with all your heart."

Today I want to spend some time unpacking what it means for us to love God. We know something about loving our neighbors. We have developed the notion of loving ourselves into a fine art. But loving God comes first, as our greatest obligation and our primary goal. What does it mean?

The law teaches us, "You shall love the Lord your God *with all your soul*." In Hebrew thought, the soul is the breath of life, the part of us that is the breathing part. One day, goes the story in Genesis, God scooped up some mud by the river bank, formed it into a human figure, and breathed into its nostrils. The statue became a being. The elements became a person. The breath of God blew alive a human soul.

To love God with the soul, therefore, is to love God with every breath. We affirm that the source of every breath is the God who gives it. We breathe because God has breathed life into us. We have the capacity to love God because God first loved us. By commanding us to love him with our soul and breath, God commands us to do what only God has made possible for us to do.

Back in the fourth century, some Christian monks visualized this insight in a memorable way. They talked about prayer as a breathing exercise. "As you inhale," they taught, "thank God for the gifts which are given you for today. As you exhale, tell God how you are going to use those gifts."

For example, breathe in and say, "I thank you, God, for daily bread." Breathe out and say, "God, let me find strength in daily bread to do the work you have given me." Breathe in and pray, "I thank you, Lord, for the forgiveness of my sins." Breathe out and pray, "I ask you, Lord, to make me a forgiving person." Breathe in, breathe out. The early monks said, "Let every breath be a prayer."

Our breath is always the power behind every word and song. There's a dear friend of mine who can be a difficult house guest. We love one another deeply, but he has an annoying habit. From the moment he opens his eyes in the morning, my friend Guy sings church hymns at the top of his lungs. He prefers loud Welsh hymns in minor keys, although sometimes he changes keys and does not know it.

It has been said of some singers that what they may lack in tone quality, they compensate in volume. The last time Guy stayed in our home, he woke me at 6:45 one Saturday morning by blasting out, "O God of earth and altar ...." Over a bleary-eyed cup of coffee, I put our friendship on the line by asking, "Why do you belt out a hymn when you wake up?" And he replied, "Haven't

41

you heard it said, 'You shall love the Lord your God with all your soul?' "

The commandment goes on to say, "You shall love the Lord your God with all your mind." We have heads to think, ideas to develop, and thoughts to express. When we wake each day we are called upon to love the Lord with our minds.

Anybody who was listening closely to the scripture lesson did not hear these words from the original commandment in Deuteronomy. The Gospel of Mark implies that Jesus added them. This gospel was written for a world that spoke Greek, in a culture with a deep respect for the human intellect and its capacity to think. If we are called upon to love God with every possible human ability, the implications are clear for the first audience of the Gospel of Mark: we are to love God with our minds.

This has always been a Jewish notion as well. A minister was getting acquainted with the newest clergyman in town, who was a rabbi at the local synagogue. Somewhat ignorant of a different religious tradition, the minister asked the rabbi how he spent his time. "I do the same things any clergy person does," he replied, "like visit the hospitals, plan programs, and deal with finances. But the most important thing my congregation pays me to do is to study."

It was a reminder to every religious leader how easy it is to get caught up in the busyness of congregational life and forget we are called to love God intelligently and intellectually. That is the business of theology. As a seminary professor once put it, "If we take seriously the notion that, in Jesus Christ, God became a human being who experienced human life, then Christians are called to think theologically about everything, from the environmental crisis to last night's sitcom." It's not enough to have a faith that feels deep feelings. We must develop a faith that thinks profound thoughts.

One of the saddest things we ever see is the person whose faith has faltered due to the malnutrition of the mind. Picture a woman in the hospital who is very sick with a lung disease. She is connected by plastic tubes to various machines. A thick clipboard is hooked to the foot of the bed. Once she had been a member of a church, but she had drifted away. A chaplain stopped to see her. Although she wasn't dying, the woman had many questions about death. As they talked, the chaplain noticed the reading material by her bed. There was a tabloid featuring a cover story on reincarnation, and a cheap magazine that told about the past lives of soap opera stars. One paper cited a recent Elvis appearance. Another made wild claims about strange visitors from another planet. Tragically, there wasn't a Bible in sight, nor any book of substance or depth. The sick woman was a prisoner to the silly whims of pop culture.

"You shall love the Lord with all your mind." If the only mental stimulation we receive comes from *People* magazine or *Wheel of Fortune*, then we do not have the capacity to know how deeply God loves us. If we're trying to handle adult life with a third-grade Sunday School education, we will not have the skills needed to negotiate the daily difficulties. As John Calvin once noted, if we are fearful, it is because we have not studied and learned the promises of God, because anxious people "do not concede the care of the world to God."[1]

The answer? There are a lot of answers. Go to an adult education class in your church. Visit a church library and take out a book that stretches your brain and fires up your imagination. Check out a commentary on a book from the Bible and work through it, verse by verse. Blessed is the person who seeks to love God through the labor of the human brain. As the apostle Paul described this mental work, "We destroy arguments and every proud obstacle raised up against the knowledge of God, and we take every thought captive in obedience to Christ" (2 Corinthians 10:4-5). To that end, we are called to love God with the mind.

To sum it up so far, "You shall love the Lord your God with all your heart," with the center of passion and trust. "You shall love the Lord your God with your soul," with the breath of life that God gives. "You shall love the Lord your God with your mind," with the brain that pursues truth. Finally, "You shall love the Lord your God with all your strength."

We misunderstand love if we reduce it to a sentiment of the heart, a word from the breath, or a thought from the mind. Love is also something we do. Love is a word that taps our energy and flexes our muscles.

There is a young man who didn't know that when he first got married. He had to be taught. He said to his new wife, "I love you." He felt it and believed it. But he didn't do anything about it. He dropped dirty socks on the floor and said, "Honey, I love you." He promised to cook supper, but arrived home an hour too late, apologizing with the words, "I love you." He promised to balance the checkbook, but didn't get around to it until three or four checks bounced. Then he expressed his regrets, adding, "I love you."

One day his wife said, "You must stop saying that you love me." He complained, "But I *do* love you. I feel it; I say it; I think it."

She said, "No, if you loved me, you would do something about it. You would keep your part of the relationship." She was right, because she knows the full shape of love.

To love God with all our strength is to keep our part of the relationship that God has established. We are called to do the tasks which God has made it possible for us to do. In this text, the kind of love called for is a love that can be commanded. Each day we wake to face some task for God's sake. If we pledge each new morning to love God with all of our strength, we pray that the work we do will be part of God's work, that we might delight in his ways and walk with his love.

What should we say when we roll out of bed? Someone paraphrases the commandment by saying, "Love the Lord God with all your passion and prayer and intelligence and energy."[2] Those are good words to put on our lips. With them we announce that our lives will be directed, not wasted. Rather than stumble around each day and end up nowhere, the Great Commandment calls us to aim our hearts and minds somewhere. As we inscribe these words upon our hearts, we aim ourselves in love toward the God who first loved us.

---

1. William J. Bouwsma, *John Calvin: A Sixteenth Century Portrait* (New York: Oxford University Press, 1988), p. 39.

2. Eugene H. Peterson, *The Message: The New Testament in Contemporary Language* (Colorado Springs, CO: NavPress, 1993), p. 120.

Commitment
Beyond Calculation

Here she is again: the widow who goes up to the temple treasury to put in her two cents. Every year she shows up at stewardship time. Teachers and preachers love to point and say, "Look at her! Truly I tell you, she has put in more than all the others."

That is not literally true, of course. In terms of quantity, many people in that line put a lot more money in the temple offering. Certainly she has earned a reputation through the centuries as a good example of sacrificial giving. Yet I have a hunch this anonymous woman would be embarrassed by the recognition she has received in thousands of stewardship sermons.

The fact is, this woman is one of the nameless saints in the Gospel of Mark. She stands in the same company with two other anonymous women. The first had a hemorrhage, and touched the cloak of Jesus to get well. The other anointed Jesus for death by breaking open a costly bottle of perfume. Like them, this woman comes out of the shadows for a moment and then disappears just as suddenly. We don't know much about her. Was she old or young? Did she have a house full of children or did she rock an empty cradle? We don't know where she lived, what she did with her days, or what kind of support she received from the extended family. Mark suggests only three details about her. First, she was a widow.

Second, she was poor. And third, she gave everything she had as a gift to support her place of worship.

Ever since, the question before the church is whether or not we will keep her on our list of saints. Is she really the kind of role model we wish to hold up?

What does she give? Two *lepta*, or two copper coins. The total value in today's currency is about a penny. That is not much. Once in a while, some treasury department official spreads a rumor about removing pennies from United States currency. Apparently pennies are too small and insignificant to matter much.

In a hungry, hurting world, small donations cannot make much of an impact. Ever see those fund-raising boxes by the cash registers of supermarkets and pizza shops? They are always full of pennies and nickels. How can any charitable organization address the great problems of the world if all it receives is small change? How can the church afford to reach out in mission if it nods to an impoverished woman and says, "Give like her!"

At least, that's what I was told a few years ago at a fund-raising seminar for non-profit organizations. The flyer promised churches a new approach to stewardship. Instead it offered savvy wisdom on fund-raising. The instructor said, "Forget about the two-penny widows or the fixed-income people. Don't give them a pledge card. Don't include them in your fund drive. They cannot give much, so it's a waste of time to go chasing after them for money. What they might give will hardly cover the time and effort you expend in chasing after them."

The instructor said, "If you want to raise funds for your non-profit organization, go after the bigger fish in your sea. Develop a relationship with the wealthiest people you know. Invite them to serve on your board. Cultivate their interest. After all, those who give the most have the greatest capacity to increase their gifts." It was sound fund-raising advice, especially in a world that values wealth, status, and prestige.

Then I went back to the church I served. I looked around the table where our official board met. Four widows served as elders that year. None of them had deep pockets or great resources, but each made sacrificial gifts to the congregation. So much for advice from fund-raisers in the world outside the church. In here, in the church, we have different values. We believe every person has infinite worth. Everybody *counts,* regardless of who they are or how much money they have. We can point to the poor widow and say, "Her gift matters, because she herself matters."

Nevertheless, that does not mean we want to look at the woman in this story as our good example for generous giving. Her presence is a troubling presence. By giving her two tarnished coins, she gives proportionally more than the rest of us.

One election year, the press disclosed the generosity of all the candidates in a presidential campaign. In the year before the campaign, Gary Hart gave a total of $140 to all charitable causes. Jesse Jackson, an advocate for the poor, gave a total of $500 to charity, even though his taxable income was well over $100,000. Ronald Reagan, who advocated that private citizens should pick up the slack of slashed welfare programs, gave only $2000 to all charitable causes, this on an income of several hundred thousand dollars. The highest giver was Walter Mondale, who gave around $13,500 to benevolences, out of an income of $500,000.[1]

Some people were outraged that misers and hypocrites were running for public office. Perhaps they shouldn't have been surprised. The giving patterns of these politicians are typical for most Americans. Many of us calculate what it takes to live each week and then donate a little piece of what's left. We give a portion of what we think we can afford. Then we want the IRS to take note of every cent.

But this nameless woman in the Gospel of Mark sees her contribution differently. She gives her money, but not in order to receive some service in return. Her contribution has nothing to do with getting a tax break. She does not calculate the monthly budget and then decide what she can afford to give out of what's left. Rather she gives it all, and then she has to figure out how she is going to live. She is committed beyond all calculation. That is troubling, for it reveals a faith so sacrificial that it scares us to death. Anybody here want to give your money like she gave hers? It would be like giving away your very life!

A minister in Gary, Indiana, tells about a woman who came out of the shadows on a Sunday morning just as the worship service was coming to an end. She had two little boys in tow, and told the usher that she wanted to talk to the pastor. Not only that, she wanted to pay her tithe.

The usher said, "You're not a member of our church. You don't have to give us any money." The woman insisted. After the benediction, she was taken up front, where she sat in the front pew and spoke with the minister. After spending a few nights with her sons in a battered women's shelter, she was taking the bus to Atlanta the next morning to start a new life far away from her abusing husband. She was leaving behind her friends and family. She had made arrangements to live in a shelter until she could find a job, get back in school, or somehow get her life in order.

"Before I leave," she said, "I want to have you pray for me, and I want to pay my tithe." She pulled out all the money she had in the world, counted out ten percent of it, and handed it to the stunned pastor. The total was $30.56. "You can't give this to us," protested the pastor. "You need it. It can make a difference for you and your boys."

"You don't understand," said the woman. "Even if I kept that ten percent, I wouldn't have enough money to provide for me and my sons. So I want to give it to God. I trust God will give me a new life. To show him I trust him, I want to give my money."

With that, the pastor took the money. Then she found a Bible to give to the woman, and prayed with her.[2]

Calling the disciples together, Jesus pointed and said, "Look at that widow. Take a good, hard look." She was the kind of person the world ignores, because she had so little. Yet she was the kind of person Jesus noticed, because she gave so much. Perhaps he saw in her something of what he has always tried to get his followers to see. Here was a woman who refused to play it safe; and neither did Jesus ever play it safe. She did not, could not, hold anything back from God; neither would he. She gave away all she had; and according to the Gospel of Mark, within a few days of leaving that temple, Jesus himself would give everything away. "Look at her," he said. "Take a good, hard look . . . because her sacrifice is a picture of what you're going to see God do in me."

48

As one pastor writes,

Charity is not something that we wish to do, not some means toward an end. Rather, charity is an obligation laid upon us by the nature of God. We are charitable because we have learned that this is the way the world is now that God has entered the world in Jesus Christ. We are not charitable in order to rid ourselves of guilt, since we know we are guilty and that our guilt is not rid through our puny actions. Rather we are charitable because it is in being charitable that we are most like the extravagant God who has been charitable to us.[3]

Commitment beyond calculation. That's what God shows us in Jesus Christ. Whenever we celebrate the central mystery of faith, we affirm a mystery that is the essence of generosity.

- *Christ has died*: he has given everything he had, all he had to live on.
- *Christ is risen*: he gives us the power to stand free from all the false attachments of this age.
- *Christ will come again*: he will complete the generous acts that he has begun.

In Jesus Christ, we have seen a God who gives his very life to us. God continues to give us this gift of life, so that we can become the kind of people who give our lives for others. In the meantime, God will do whatever he can to get our attention.

In one of his Lake Wobegon stories, Garrison Keillor tells about a Sunday morning in Lake Wobegon Lutheran Church. The sermon has been droning on far too long, and Clarence Bunsen has checked out early. He realizes it's almost time for the offering, so he quietly reaches for his wallet. Upon opening his wallet, Clarence discovers he has no cash. He takes out his pen and hides the checkbook in the middle of his Bible, next to one of the psalms. He begins to scratch out a check for thirty dollars, because he almost had a heart attack that week, and because somebody in the church will count the offering and he wants them to see he gave thirty dollars.

He tries not to be obvious, but a lady to his right sees him. Clarence can tell she thinks he's writing in the pew Bible, so he doesn't look at what he's doing. She gives him a funny stare, and turns back to the sermon. Clarence tries to quietly rip the check out of the checkbook, with limited success, still not looking at what he's doing so the lady in the pew won't know he has written out a check in church. The offering plate comes by, and Clarence proudly puts in the check, only to realize a moment too late that he has just written a check for three hundred dollars. He accidently wrote three-zero-zero on two different lines when he wasn't looking.

What could he do? On the one hand, he couldn't go downstairs after church and find the deacons counting the collection and say, "Fellows, there's been a mistake. I gave more than I really wanted to." On the other hand, he gave all he had in the checking account and a little more. Perhaps he and his family will have to eat beans and oatmeal for the rest of the month, Clarence thought, even though the contribution was going to a good place. One thing was for sure, notes Keillor. In that moment, Clarence felt fully alive for the first time all day.[4]

Commitment beyond calculation. That's what God-in-Christ is watching for. The Lord has been so generous in providing every gift we need. Every day he watches to see what we do with what he has given us. We can learn something from that nameless widow whom we hear about during every stewardship season. She did not merely give her money. Instead she first pledged her heart to God, and the money went with it.

That is easier said than done. A lot of people will say, "I don't have much to give. I can't afford to be generous. I really don't have anything to offer."

Yet the promise of the gospel is sure. The Lord can do a lot with a little when he has it all.

---

1. William H. Willimon, "The Effusiveness of Christian Charity," *Theology Today* 49/1 (April 1992), p. 76.

2. Wendy Pratt, *PresbyNet Sermonshop*, November 3, 1994.

3. Willimon, p. 78.

4. Garrison Keillor, *Leaving Home* (New York: Penguin Books, 1987), pp. 90-91.

Something To Do While
The World Falls Apart

A number of years ago, leaders in a church decided to track down the congregation's drop-outs. They combed through the membership list, put together a list of names, and sent out volunteers two-by-two to knock on doors and invite the absent members back to church.

As is often the case, the volunteer visitors discovered that most of the people visited had found other things to do on Sunday morning. One person said, "I would come back to church if it didn't conflict with my tennis time." Another said, "We came to church when our kids were involved. When they outgrew Sunday School, we stopped going." Another said, "I enjoy going to church on the really big days, like Christmas, Easter, and the Fourth of July. Compared to those days, other services are a little bit dull."

One response was different. Two volunteers named Jack and Esther went to see a man whom nobody knew. He lived on the end of the street, in a big house behind three overgrown pine trees. It took the volunteers a few minutes to find the front door. All the curtains were drawn. It looked like nobody was home. Suddenly the door swung open, and a thin man with a shock of white hair said, "My name's Tarnower. What do you want?" They said, "We're from the church. We stopped by to see you." He invited them in. They explained why they had come.

In a few minutes, he was shaking a bony finger at them. "I'll tell you why I don't go to church anymore. It's because I got in the habit of reading the *Sunday Times* before I went to the worship service."

Esther leaned forward. "Tell us," she said warmly, "how did the newspaper keep you from coming to church? Did you get caught up in the sports section and lose track of time? Or the comics?"

Mr. Tarnower looked at her with wild eyes. "No," he said, "I read the news. It's an awful world out there. There are a lot of diseases I don't understand. Wars break out. Families fall apart. Children run through the streets with handguns. People die prematurely. Listen, the world is falling apart, and the church can't do a thing about it."

"Well," Jack said, "you ought to come back. We have a nice minister, a fairly good choir, and a Bible study on Wednesday nights. You might enjoy our program."

"No," Mr. Tarnower said, "I don't think so. I get out for groceries, but that's all I want to face. I went to church for a while, but the world got worse. When my wife died, I decided to sit in here, watch everything fall apart, and wait my turn. I don't go to church anymore. The church has nothing to say."

He has a point. We live in a rough and painful world that seems to grow worse each day. As Walter Brueggemann notes,

> *For all our intellectual sophistication, seemingly assured affluence and confidence in our technology, a deep, unsettled feeling that things are indeed falling apart cuts across the spectrum . . . Our best institutions seem oddly dysfunctional. Churches worry about survival, courts only sometimes yield justice, medical institutions provide sporadic access and care, schools only occasionally educate and all our institutions seem in a deep crisis of purpose as well as finances . . . and the presence and threat of violence is everywhere.*[1]

One day, four of the disciples heard Jesus speak about a world coming unglued. He told them, among other things, that the Jerusalem Temple would be destroyed. Imagine how hard that was to believe! The Temple was the central institution of Israel, the primary religious shrine, the center of commerce and banking, the heart of history and tradition. Jesus said, "The temple shall fall to the ground, stone by stone, piece by piece."

The four disciples were understandably shaken. As Jesus went on to say, his disciples will be subject to every kind of pain and abuse: wars, famines, earthquakes, persecutions, beatings, betrayals, and death. In such a world, what can anybody do?

Jesus gives his disciples something to do. He gives them a commandment, an imperative in the midst of passive language. When the world comes apart, what should every disciple do, first and foremost? Jesus says, "Preach the gospel." That is what he demands of us: *The good news must first be proclaimed to all nations.*

What a curious thing to say! When the world is falling apart, shall we stand up and deliver a sermon? Imagine if the news came that a huge asteroid was headed for the earth. There is nothing we could do. Destruction is imminent. Civilized life is about to end. Meanwhile some preacher stands up in a black Genevan gown and says, "Let me give you three points and a poem." That is a silly picture.

What does Jesus mean when he says, "When the world is falling apart, preach the gospel"? Historically speaking, some people in the church have taken that to mean, "Get as many people in the church as you can. Scare them if you must."

Every few years, someone writes yet another religious best-seller about the end of the world. The world never ends, but the books continue to be published. Each claims to be a work of "prophecy," and strings together random Bible verses that try to prove Saddam Hussein is the Great Beast, or some wild idea like that. Each chapter warns the Second Coming of Jesus will take place at any time. "The time is short," these writers say, "so turn to the back of the book, follow the Four Easy Steps, and stop worrying about the world any more. The world outside may blow apart, but at least you've got Jesus in your heart." In many books and churches, this is the point of all preaching: to escape from the world's calamities.

Should troubles come, all some people do is point to the horizon and say, "Look, there he is! Jesus is coming again." As a radio preacher once claimed, "The Bible says that when things in the world get to their absolute worst, Christians won't have to suffer through it. The trumpet will sound, and Jesus will gather all of his believers into the air and rescue them from danger. In fact, if you are a Christian who owns a car, you have a responsibility to put a bumper sticker on your car to warn those left behind that, when the trumpet sounds, your Christian car will be going out of control."[2]

Jesus warned against people like him. "Beware no one leads you astray. When you hear of wars and rumors of wars, do not be alarmed; this must take place, but the end is still a long way off. Nation will rise against nation and kingdom against kingdom; there will be earthquakes in various places; there will be famines. But this is only the beginning of the birthpangs."

Old Mr. Tarnower was right. This is a world where things fall apart. The writer of Mark's gospel knows that, perhaps more than all the other writers of the New Testament. This is a world of disease, of headaches and hemorrhages. This is a world that reminds us of our human weakness, with deafness, blindness, paralysis, and death. This is a world of deception and meanness, where people put spins on the truth and do what they can to put themselves in power over others. This is a world of chaos and cruelty, where the innocent suffer and lives are put at risk. Mark knows that.

But Mark knows something else. In the words of a favorite hymn of the church,

> And though this world, with devils filled,
> Should threaten to undo us,
> We will not fear, for God hath willed
> His truth to triumph through us.
> The prince of darkness grim, We tremble not for him;
> His rage we can endure, For lo! his doom is sure,
> One little word shall fell him . . . [3]

. . . and the Word is Jesus Christ. He is stronger than all that can hurt or destroy. That is the Word we must proclaim, the Word we must speak at all costs. The world may be haunted by evil, but it belongs to God. We may be in love with our own destruction, but we have been claimed by the strong Son of God. Even when evil and unbelief swelled up to kill him, God raised up Jesus to keep confronting his enemies, until the day they are put beneath his feet. Yes, this is a world where things fall apart. But God is stronger. God has not given up. God is going to win. That's what we have to say.

No wonder, then, Jesus said this to Simon, Andrew, James, and John. They walked with him ever since he said, "The time is fulfilled; God's kingdom is at hand. Turn and believe the good news" (Mark 1:15). They saw that kingdom advance one step at a time. The tormented person found peace. The eyes of the blind were opened. The ears of the deaf were unstopped. The lame person jumped like a deer. The tongues of the speechless sang for joy.

In other words, preaching the kingdom is always more than speaking a Word. It is *kerygma*, a proclamation, a Word proclaimed in speech and action. It is doing mission. As one scholar notes, "This preaching is more than the poetic eloquence of gifted public speech. This preaching was the eschatological realization, the making immediate, of the kingdom of God."[4]

In Jesus Christ, God's reign has broken in. The four disciples wanted to know, "When will the kingdom come?" as if it were a distant, glorious age. But the church cannot ponder the arrival of the coming age as if it were a bus running behind schedule. We are given the task of proclaiming what God has begun in Jesus Christ. The faithful Christian never sits on a mountain to await the Second Coming. No, our job is to take seriously Christ's First Coming. The time of the Second Coming is none of our business, but it is our business to act as if the world has changed because of Jesus Christ. We are called to do what Christ does: to proclaim God's reign in word and deed, to act as if the times have changed, to believe and behave as if God rules over every opposing power.

There is a funeral at the end of one of Frederick Buechner's novels. It may be the only way the story could come to a close. A lot of terrible things happen in the book. Theodore Nicolet, a Protestant minister, loses his wife in a car accident. He is left to raise two small girls with the help of a housekeeper, Irma Reinwasser, who is a Holocaust survivor. One day he goes to track down a wayward church member who left her husband. That piques the interest of the editor of the town newspaper. He doesn't have a lot of news that week. So he takes the opportunity to print a few rumors about Nicolet's pastoral care. None are true, but the damage is done. Nicolet returns home, reunites the woman with her husband, and does what he can to set the record straight. Irma speaks up for him. "He's a good man. Leave him alone."

Irma dies shortly thereafter. A few teenagers are caught up in the public spectacle, and decide to pull a prank on her. Her house catches fire and she dies. So, at the end of the book, the whole town gathers around the grave of Irma Reinwasser. Nicolet read the words from the book of Revelation: "And God shall wipe away all tears, and there shall be no more death, neither sorrow, nor crying, neither shall there be any more pain, for the former things have passed away" (Revelation 21:4).

He spoke for a few minutes, then concluded with words of committal and a benediction. The people began to shuffle away in the rain. One turned back. It was Will Poteat, the sleazy newspaper editor who caused the turmoil while Nicolet was out of town. "Good show," he said to the preacher. Then he pointed to the grave and sneered, "This supper of the great God . . . no more death, no more pain. Ask her."

Nicolet stood silent, his two daughters by his side. He didn't know what to say. He didn't know what to do. Suddenly his daughters did an unexpected thing.

> *They grabbed up some of the flowers that they had brought and started pelting him with them — orange hawkweed, daisies, clover —- and stooping over like a great, pale bear in his baggy seersucker suit, he kept on lunging at them with his finger. Nicolet threw back his head and laughed as Poteat went lumbering off with the little girls after him. When he got as far as Nicolet's car, he turned around for a moment, and it was only then that they could see that he was more or less laughing himself.*[5]

What do you do when the world falls apart? "Preach the kingdom," says Jesus to all his followers. Even if life should turn deadly, we proclaim the power of God that is stronger than death. And preach and proclaim we shall, until the day when there are no more tears, when death has no more power, when grief is swallowed up in laughter.

1. Walter Brueggemann, "The terrible ungluing," *The Christian Century* 21 October 1992.

2. I wish this were a fictional story, but a radio announcer in eastern Pennsylvania actually made this claim in the fall of 1994.

3. *Presbyterian Hymnal* (Louisville: Westminster/John Knox Press, 1990), p. 260.

4. Brian Blount, "Preaching the Kingdom: Mark's Apocalyptic Call for Prophetic Engagement," *Princeton Theological Seminary Bulletin* Supplementary Issue, Number 3 (June 1994), p. 46.

5. Frederick Buechner, *The Final Beast* (San Francisco: Harper and Row, 1965), p. 276.

When All Is
Said And Done

The Jehovah's Witnesses have changed their minds. After warning for decades that the world would end within this present generation, the leaders of the sect announced in December 1995 that they have softened their position. As a spokesman explained, "Jesus said that 'this generation will not pass away' until a number of signs have taken place (Mark 13:30). When we reflected on the scriptures, we decided that he was talking about his generation rather than ours."

Ex-Witness James Fenton, professor emeritus at the University of Lethbridge in Alberta, Canada, is pleased by the change in doctrine. The Witnesses probably won't be knocking on our doors, he notes. The reason for their urgency no longer exists. Since the Jehovah's Witnesses have officially declared that the world probably will not end tomorrow, they will have a harder time motivating their members to ring more doorbells and gather more followers.[1]

What that means, of course, is that the Jehovah's Witnesses are now like many of the rest of us. We have grown relaxed in our anticipation for the end of the world. Much of the New Testament was written by a church that lived on tiptoe, always watching for the imminent return of Jesus Christ. As time passed, the urgency cooled. As one generation after another passed away, the church found it difficult to maintain much enthusiasm for the end of the world.

This lack of fervor is not supported by a silence within the Bible. The Jewish and Christian scriptures frequently speak of a final consummation of human history. Life had a beginning. Life will have an end. The prophets spoke of the "day of the Lord," a final day when God will come in judgment and justice. The early church identified the end with the second coming of the risen Jesus, who will return to vindicate and complete what he started. Speaking of that day, Jesus said, "They will see 'the Son of Man coming in clouds' with great power and glory" (Mark 13:26).

Yet we wait for this to happen. As we wait, we grow tired. As we grow tired, we let our culture tell its own story about the way the world will end.

As a grade school student in the '60s, I was well trained in duck and cover drills. Once a month an alarm would sound. Our teachers paraded us into the hallway. Then they told us to sit on the tile floor and cover our heads with our arms.

Duck and cover drills seemed especially urgent in our school. The playground at Washington Gladden Elementary overlooked the IBM plant where most of our fathers worked. In the '60s, while other divisions of IBM were busy developing mainframe computers, the plant in my home town worked on undisclosed projects for the government. Years later, when the Cold War thawed, my father filled in a few gaps. It seems that during the '60s, while my friends and I were playing on swing sets and jungle gyms, people at IBM were developing computer guidance systems for bombers, tactical warning systems, and top secret surveillance equipment.

One day in third grade the alarm sounded. We moved to the hall and assumed the position. I sat at the feet of two teachers who had a conversation that scared me deeply. "I don't know why we do this," the first teacher said. The second said, "The kids need to be prepared in case the Russians drop the bomb." "Listen," said the first. "Rumor has it that we are half a mile from ground zero. The IBM plant down the hill is on the top ten list for Russia's targets. If they ever drop the bomb, none of us will ever get the chance to duck and cover."

By the time most children get to third grade, they have heard the story of Chicken Little. The fearful little bird gets bonked on the head and cries, "The sky is falling! The sky is falling!" When the truth is told, kids laugh at the story. Most third graders have also seen a cartoon of a sandwich board prophet who announces, "The end is near!" They have learned from adults that such people are probably crackpots and cranks, and not to be taken seriously. But sitting in a grade school hallway, it occurred to me for the first time that the world as I knew it might actually come to an end.

In today's text, Jesus affirms that this world will come to an end. That's a truth that I learned in third grade, not in church. If anything, church was a place where it seemed like the world was going to go on forever. Yet I will never forget that moment, not in church but in school, when it became clear that we lived under the shadow of a mushroom cloud. Who knows if the teacher was feeling cynical about the safety drill or hopeless about our common future? Either way, he knew there was a chance this world might be blown to atomic smithereens. For the first time, I knew it, too.

We don't have a lot of American elementary schools that still do duck and cover drills. It is probably a different story in places like Bosnia, Belfast, or the Sudan, where lives are on the line and few children would laugh at the story of Chicken Little. In most of the world's trouble spots, no one doubts that one bomb or one stray bullet could blow apart somebody's world in a matter of seconds. Many people live with potential destruction every day of their lives.

Yet when all is said and done, the church believes that this is not how the world is going to end.

One day Jesus and his disciples came out of the Temple in Jerusalem. One of the twelve turned around, looked up at the high towers and the massive blocks of stone, and, with the tone of a small town hick on his first trip to Manhattan, said, "Golly, Jesus! That's an amazing building." Jesus replied, "Do you see these great buildings? One day, they're going to be torn down and scattered like children's blocks." They looked at Jesus in terrified astonishment. The Temple was the central house of worship for an entire nation, the spiritual home for all scattered Jews. It symbolized

63

the meeting place where God came to dwell with his people. How could Jesus talk about its demolition?

A little while later, four of them pulled him aside and said, "Jesus, what exactly are you talking about?" That began a grim recital of events in the thirteenth chapter of Mark, from which we heard a piece today. Looking ahead, Jesus spoke of earthquakes, wars and rumors of wars, famines, persecution, betrayal, and suffering. "That's how it's going to be," said Jesus, because in some sense, that's the way it is. If we doubt it, we can pick up a newspaper and read it for ourselves.

The key to this passage, however, is that Jesus does not speak about the end of the world, as much as he speaks of a *world that is coming to an end*. One hopes we can hear the difference. For, in a world like this, human institutions like the Temple crumble apart stone by stone. It seems an inevitable part of this age. But Jesus claims this worn-out world is passing away.

In a world like this, there are people who stand up to tell the truth, who speak good news, and who point to what God is doing. As a result, they are abused, beaten down, and betrayed by those close at hand. That's how it is in this age; but this old world is passing away.

In a world like this, there are drive-by shootings, acts of verbal abuse, and children who have nightmares about atomic clouds. But the good news is that this weary, old world is passing away. "Don't be alarmed," Jesus says, "for in a world like this, you can always expect nation against nation, kingdom against kingdom. The good news is that the end of all this fighting is in sight."

The evidence is found in his own words, as Jesus speaks of signs that we have already seen fulfilled. Even as we wait for the end of the world, Christians are those people who have, in a sense, already seen the end of the world. We have seen it in the cross. Jesus promised, "The sun will be darkened, and the moon will not give its light, and the stars will be falling from heaven." A short time after he said it, darkness came over the whole land on a Friday afternoon from noon until three (Mark 15:33), and the lights of the heavens were extinguished, exactly as he said. Then Jesus said, "The powers in the heavens will be shaken." Shortly thereafter,

Jesus breathed his last on the cross, and "the curtain of the temple was ripped in two, from top to bottom" (Mark 15:38). According to Mark, it happened with the same force as the day of his baptism, when God ripped apart the sky (Mark 1:10). The powers were shaken, just as he promised.

The clearest sign, according to Jesus, was that people would "see the Son of Man." All who looked upon the cross saw him plain as day, in power and glory. As scholar Ched Myers points out, "In Mark's story the cross is neither a heroic nor a tragic moment. It is an *apocalyptic* one, the epiphany of a new power that 'shakes the Powers in the heavens.' "[2] The death of Jesus killed off the world as we've known it. In the suffering of Jesus, the old world of brutality passed away. A whole new creation was born.

The challenge for us in these difficult times is to live toward that new world as if it's already here. Christians are people who live as if the times have changed. We wait for the Son of Man to come again because we have seen the Son of Man in the power of the cross. We watch for his future kingdom because, in the death of Jesus, God's kingdom is *already* here. We continue to wait, because the kingdom is *not yet* here. Not completely. We live in the tension between "already" and "not yet."

It isn't easy standing on one foot and then another. We trust God's will ultimately, yet we cope with unfinished suffering. The stakes are high and it's easy to give in. Neill Hamilton, who taught at Drew University for many years, once observed how people in our time lose hope for the future. It happens whenever we let our culture call the shots on how the world is going to end. At this stage of technological advancement, the only way the culture can make sense of the future is through the picture of everything blowing up in a nuclear holocaust. The world cannot know what we know, that everything has changed in the death and resurrection of Jesus, that the same Christ is coming to judge the world and give birth to a new creation. And so, people lose hope. As Hamilton puts it:

> *This substitution of an image of nuclear holocaust for the coming of Christ is a parable of what happens to Christians when they cease to believe in their own*

eschatological heritage. The culture supplies its own images for the end when we default by ceasing to believe in biblical images of God's triumph at the end.[3]

The good news of the gospel is this: when all is said and done, God is going to win. We are invited to live as if God's final victory is a done deal. But can we believe it?

Iwan Russell-Jones recently asked why so many wild-eyed prophets of the future end up as television preachers. In the world of religious broadcasting, you have to look long and hard to find a reasonable and faithful voice.

To take one example, he observed an evangelist named Jack Van Impe and his wife Rexella, two figures who were made for television. Their hairstyles defy the laws of gravity, their teeth are unreasonably numerous and white, and they know and love us all individually. Their weekly show, *Jack Van Impe Presents*, purports to look at world events through the eyes of faith. Contrary to Jesus' warnings in Mark 13, Jack and Rexella point to news items as if they are cogs in God's mechanical plan for the future. This is highly speculative theology, says Russell-Jones, as these evangelists list one earthquake after another famine, and declare "It's God's unfolding will!" Whether Jack and Rexella realize it, their scenarios are also unabashedly pro-American. In all of their end-of-the-world schemes, the devastation and carnage takes place in other countries, apparently so Americans can watch it on television.

It's easy for us mainline folks to take shots at Jack and his wife Rexella, particularly when it comes to their silly and simplistic views of the future. But what do we have? Could it be that, just maybe, we have given in to the despair and hopelessness of our culture? Have we given up on God's future, left with a hand-wringing pessimism about the state of the world? Have we felt abandoned by God? Jack and Rexella would answer, "Of course not! We are preparing for the coming of Christ our Lord."

So why don't people like us have a place on the religious airwaves? Iwan Russell-Jones admits, "It's difficult to make a mark in the communications business when you don't have anything much to say." Then he concludes:

The time for us sensible, "mainline" folk to make a serious move into the world of television will be when we can pray with Jack and Rexella "Even so, come quickly, Lord Jesus." And mean it.[4]

---

1. John Dart, "Jehovah's Witnesses Abandon End-of-the-world Prediction," *Religious News Service* 1 December 1995, PresbyNet, p. 3318.

2. Ched Myers, *Who Will Roll Away the Stone? Discipleship Queries for First World Christians* (Maryknoll, NY: Orbis Books, 1994), p. 249.

3. Neill Q. Hamilton, *Maturing in the Christian Life: A Pastor's Guide* (Philadelphia: The Geneva Press, 1984), p. 68.

4. Iwan Russell-Jones, "Jack Van Impe Presents," *Journal for Preachers* (Lent 1994), pp. 25-29.

Liberating Truth

During the 1960s, Sherwood Schwartz wrote and produced a number of hit television shows. One of the most popular shows was *Gilligan's Island*, a comedy about a handful of pleasure cruise passengers who found themselves shipwrecked on a desert island. Every episode featured the castaways of the *S.S. Minnow* facing a wacky new adventure. The show was an immediate hit of the 1964 season. Each week, a lot of otherwise thoughtful, intelligent television viewers tuned in to hear the Skipper say, "Gilligan, drop those coconuts!"

Schwartz says only six episodes had gone on the air when a commander of the United States Coast Guard marched into his office. The commander handed over a stack of about two dozen telegrams he had received. Each telegram basically said the same thing: "For several weeks now, we have seen American citizens stranded on some Pacific island. Why doesn't the Coast Guard do something about it? Can't you send a U.S. destroyer to rescue those shipwrecked people before they starve to death?" Believe it or not, absolutely none of the telegrams were jokes. They came from viewers who were deeply concerned about the people they saw on that imaginary television show.[1]

A lot of us can laugh at a story like that. We believe we know the difference between fact and fiction. Most of the time we can distinguish between the fantasy of a Thursday night sitcom and the reality of daily life. A thirty-minute show may look better, or sound funnier, but sooner or later somebody turns off the television and we take life for what it is. Each new day dawns with its own distance and perspective. In the words of Jesus, "You will know the truth and the truth will make you free."

It's no wonder this famous one-liner from the Gospel of John has been inscribed in the cornerstones of schools and the entryways of public libraries. For us, the pursuit of truth has often been the business of education. We go to school, not simply to have our heads filled with facts both useless and useful, but to have an encounter with truth. A good education can open our minds and purge us of a lot of illusions. A college freshman said, "I was number two in my high school class. After I unpacked my bags at college, I discovered that everybody in my dormitory had been number one in their high school classes. Then I went to a freshman English class with a hundred other students, and I learned I wasn't half as smart as everybody always told me I was." Now, there's a teachable soul — even if the truth was hard to swallow.

"You will know the truth." That's the promise Jesus gave his disciples in today's text. It seems like an appropriate word as we remember the Protestant Reformation. Much of the Reformation began as an educational movement. The early sixteenth century was the high water mark of the Renaissance. People began thinking for themselves. The printing press made the Bible available to people on a wide scale and gave them something to think about. No longer were the clergy the sole keepers of knowledge. As lay people began to study and ponder the Bible, they discovered their place in the priesthood of Christ. As one of my seminary professors once said, "Once people wise up, they never wise down." After all, the truth sets people free.

At least we would hope so. The fact is, the word "truth" is a loaded term for the Gospel of John. John says the very essence of the good news of Jesus Christ is "grace and truth" (John 1:14). According to this writer, the single watershed event in the history of the world is the coming of Jesus Christ into the world. On the one hand, it is a disclosure of sheer grace. The incarnation announces that God is recklessly, relentlessly inclined in our favor, that "God so loved the world that he sent his only Son." Yet on the other hand, the coming of Christ is also a disclosure about ourselves. Jesus reveals the truth about who we are and who we are not. In Jesus, truth comes down to a world of falsehood, just as light breaks into a world of darkness. Either way you look at it, truth and light both mean exposure, and honesty, and stripping away every pretense. Sometimes people wise up, and somebody else will wish they hadn't. It can be very painful.

A priest in the inner city wanted to help some neighborhood kids. He wanted them to see something more than their own situations. So he put them on a bus and took them to see some things of great beauty. They went to the art museum and saw paintings by the masters. They went to a symphony matinee and heard beautiful music. They went for a walk through a row of homes that were done over by a creative team of architects. That young priest showed those kids the best and brightest things he knew. Then they climbed back on the bus and went home. That night one of those kids set his apartment house on fire. Nobody was harmed, but the place burned down. The priest was in tears when he visited the boy in jail. "Why did you do it?" he asked.

The boy said, "Today I saw all those beautiful things. I was caught up in their glory. Then I came home and saw how ugly my world was, and I hated it, and I wanted to burn it down." He saw the truth, and it provoked violence and destruction.

When Jesus spoke in today's gospel lesson, he was standing in the thick of a nasty debate with leaders of the Jerusalem temple. They were calling him names. They challenged his sanity. They disputed his family background. In the face of meanness, Jesus said, "If you knew the truth, it would make you free."

His opponents roared, "We are children of Abraham. We have never been slaves to anyone. How can you talk about freedom?"

Jesus stared them down and said, "You don't see it, but you're slaves, all right. You think you are already free, but you're not. You believe your religious affiliation will save you, but it won't. You think if *you* keep working hard and doing what *you* think is right, it will glorify God and make your life better. Yet even now you try to kill me, a man who has told you the God-given truth. That's not freedom; that's a kind of slavery and you're stuck in it. The pitiful thing is you don't know any better, even though you think you know better."

What Jesus was getting at, I think, is just how pervasive are the illusions we live under. When we think we have a corner on the truth, our words and deeds may be opposed to God. If we dare to tell one another, "I know what I'm doing," there's always evidence that we don't do everything God wants us to do. We think we are free, yet we really aren't free. As someone once quipped, "Those who believe they are liberated may merely be unzipped."

We live under a lot of illusions. One illusion in our time is that a good education will make us better people. In some ways, it might. But an education provides no assurance we will be more obedient or truthful. Neither can we expect schooling to guarantee peace of mind or unity among enemies.

The southern novelist Walker Percy was trained as a physician. His medical training gave him the ability to diagnose a variety of diseases which reflect a deeper malaise in our culture. In one of his articles, he noted:

> *The deeper we get into the century, the more sense people make, but they are making different kinds of senses which don't compute with each other. Carl Sagan explains everything without God, from the most distant galaxies to our own individual nastiness, which is caused by our reptilian brains. Radio and TV preachers explain everything by God, (our) happiness with God, (our) unhappiness without God. Humanists explain everything by coming out for the freedom and dignity of the individual. One hundred million books have been written by psychotherapists on how to be creative and self-fulfilling. And here's this nice ordinary American who works hard all day and is watching his six hours of TV and his wife is reading **The National Enquirer** and is more likely to set store by astrology and psychics than by science or God. The slaughter and the terror of the century continues. And people are, by and large, nicer*

than ever ... It is a peculiar time, indeed, when a writer
doesn't know who the enemy is, or, even worse, when he
can't stand his friends.[2]

Is there a way out? Is there some truth that will make us free? These questions haunted an Augustinian monk named Martin Luther. After a close call with a lightning bolt in the year 1505, he entered a monastery and took the vows. For a dozen years or so, he tried to work out his salvation with fear and trembling. He did whatever he could to be a righteous person.

The problem was that, no matter how hard he tried, Luther was never good enough. He was never free from himself. One biographer tells us that Luther confessed his sins almost daily, sometimes for as long as six hours in a single sitting. He believed every sin to be forgiven must be confessed, and every sin to be confessed must first be remembered. So he spent hours trying to remember the truth about his life, recalling every wayward thought and dirty deed, both real and anticipated. As a memory device, he repeated the list of seven deadly sins, one at a time, and tried to recall every occasion when he had felt an inclination to commit each sin. He recited the Ten Commandments, line by line, and then probed his own heart to remember every time he broke, or thought about breaking, God's Law. Those assigned to listen to Brother Luther's sins often grew weary. "Look here," someone once said to him, "if you expect Christ to forgive you, come in here with something to forgive — murder, blasphemy, adultery — instead of all these peccadilloes."[3]

Luther knew better. He was a prisoner of sin. To think otherwise was, and is, an illusion. His whole life was saturated with sin, even in the relative protection of the monastery. On every page of his Bible, he found something that judged his life and condemned his soul.

Yet, as you know, something happened. Martin Luther discovered there were other things in his Bible. In 1515, he began to lecture some students on the book of Romans. Like every good teacher, he learned something when he taught. When he flipped to the third chapter of Romans, he knew it said, "All have sinned and fall short of the glory of God." He knew it was there; that was his burden. But then he stumbled over the next verse, where it says, "All are now justified by his grace as a gift, through the redemption that is in Christ Jesus" (Romans 3:23-24).

The next year, Luther began to lecture on the book of Galatians. When he got to the second chapter, he knew what it was going to say. He read, "A person is not justified by the works of the law," and he groaned, because that was the burden of truth. For years, Martin Luther tried to keep God's Law and it was killing him. Then he read, "And we have come to believe in Christ Jesus, so that we might be justified by faith in Christ" (Galatians 2:16). That was it! That was the way out of every illusion, falsehood, and sin: through faith in the Christ who sets us free.

You see, it's one thing to go looking for the truth. Sometimes we think if we keep seeking long enough, we will find the truth. Or if we go to enough schools we will find the one idea that unlocks the door to freedom. Or if we keep practicing our religious habits, we will glimpse the one insight we have been missing. Yet the central truth of the gospel is neither a proposition nor an idea. It is not a perspective, an overarching scheme, or the hidden structure behind all reality. The truth is a person named Jesus. He himself says, "I am the truth" (John 14:6). He is not only the way and the life; he is the truth. We do not have to go looking for him, because he has already found us. He gave his life for us, thus bridging any gap between what God expects of us and what we can achieve. In his death, Christ has justified us in God's sight. In the power of his resurrection, he invites us to abide in his freedom.

"You will know the truth and the truth will make you free." We know this liberating truth when we affirm what God has done in Jesus Christ. When we were prisoners of sin and captives to the powers of death, God sent Jesus to save us and set us free. This is the truth about the One who is the truth, and it makes all the difference in the world. Jesus himself said so: "If the Son makes you free, you will be free indeed" (John 8:36).

_____

1. As reported by William F. Fore, *Television and Religion: The Shaping of Faith, Values, and Culture* (Minneapolis: Augsburg Publishing House, 1987), p. 55.

2. Walker Percy, *Signposts in a Strange Land* (New York: Farrar, Straus, and Giroux, 1991), pp. 159-160.

3. Roland H. Bainton, *Here I Stand: A Life of Martin Luther* (Nashville: Abingdon Press, 1950), p. 41.

Tears At
The Tomb

By all appearances, the junior high youth group at First Church was going well. Bob and Betsy, their two enthusiastic advisors, planned a full calendar of events to keep them busy. The youth went to roller skating parties and winter retreats. They played a variety of sports, discussed a lot of movies, and celebrated every holiday with a party. But when it came to leading the young teens into the deeper waters of faith, Bob and Betsy were frustrated.

One Sunday afternoon, Bob announced the group was beginning a study of the Gospel of John. "It's a good book," he said, "and we think a church youth group should read it." To begin the study, he gave the kids an assignment. "During the next week," Bob said, "we want you to flip through the Gospel of John until you find a verse that means something to you. Memorize the verse. Next week, come back and recite it for the rest of the group."

Attendance the next week was spotty, but the few who were present were also prepared. They went around the circle, starting with Diane. "My verse is John 3:16," Diane said. "God so loved the world that he gave his only Son, so that everyone who believes in him may not perish but may have eternal life." Betsy asked why she picked the verse. Diane said, "My grandmother said it was important."

Mark was next. He quoted, "Truly, I tell you, no one can see the kingdom of God without being born from above" (John 3:3). When the advisors asked him why he selected it, Mark said, "I opened my dad's Bible and saw these words were printed in red ink. I figured they must be important."

On around the circle they went. Whether they knew it or not, the kids in the group were doing something important. The Gospel of John is full of pithy, pungent sayings, like "The Word became flesh and lived among us" (John 1:14), or "I am the resurrection and the life" (John 11:25). Every page has three or four important truths compressed like brilliant diamonds. In every chapter, the eternal Word of God is revealed not only in stories but in memorable one-liners. By memorizing these verses, in some sense those Junior Highs were learning the gospel.

At least it looked that way. Soon it was time for the last youth to speak. Jonathan was the minister's son. Grinning from a successful Bible study, Betsy said, "Jonathan, tell us what verse you have memorized today."

Jonathan said, "My verse is John 11:35."

Bob said, "Can you remember how it goes?"

"Sure," said Jonathan. He cleared his throat. He stood erect and looked around the group. Then with a note of sobriety he said, "*Jesus wept.*"

That did it. The rest of the kids burst into laughter. Bob and Betsy tried to grab the reins of those runaway wild horses. "Tell us, Jonathan," Betsy said, "why did you pick that verse?"

With perfect teenage logic, Jonathan replied, "Because it's the shortest verse in the Bible."

At first glance, that brief verse looks like a lightweight compared to other verses. The Gospel of John often reveals the eternal Word in single sentences, but the sentence "Jesus wept" does not sound like one of them. Even when the New Revised Standard Version expands it to four words ("Jesus began to weep"), John 11:35 doesn't seem to carry the full freight of the Gospel.

That brief verse occurs in the story of the death of Lazarus, a significant event in the ministry of Jesus. Lazarus was a disciple whom Jesus loved (John 11:5). More than a servant, Jesus called him "friend" (John 11:11). Yet Lazarus was dead. He was neither sleeping nor hiding out of sight. Lazarus was stone-cold in the tomb. When Jesus arrived, it was too late. If Jesus had come sooner, he might have healed the illness. But by the time Jesus reached Bethany, nothing could be done.

According to the story in John 11, the death of a beloved friend was the event that prompted Jesus' tears. His tears looked like our tears. This fact had led some commentators, and a lot of preachers, to assume Jesus was deeply moved at the death of his friend. Perhaps Jesus was overcome by grief, sentiment, and sadness at the loss of a loved one. At the tomb, Jesus appeared as human as the rest of us.

Many people are comforted by that sight. A few years ago, four-year-old Conor Clapton fell to his death in New York City. After the tragedy his father, rock guitarist Eric Clapton, said, "I turned to stone. Then I went off the edge of the world for a while." In time, Clapton put his tortured felings in a song:

> *Beyond the door, there's peace I'm sure,*
> *And I know there'll be no more tears in heaven.*[1]

In the midst of tragedy, it is a great comfort to know Jesus wept as we weep, that indeed there are tears in heaven as there are tears on earth. We want to know God is compassionate, that the Lord of Israel suffers with us. When people gathered outside the tomb of Lazarus, some saw those tears and said, "See how Jesus loved him" (John 11:36). At the point of human brokenness, it is comforting to know the Holy One sympathizes with us.

But wait a minute. Others outside the same tomb said, "Couldn't Jesus have kept his friend from dying? Isn't there something curious about these tears?" The answer to both questions, of course, was yes. Both Martha and Mary knew it. Each came independently and said, "Lord, if only you had been here, my brother would not have died." They knew his power. They knew Jesus could do whatever he wanted. But he did not prevent the death, just as he still doesn't keep people from dying.

That suggests a second possible explanation for his tears. According to the story, Jesus "was greatly disturbed in spirit and deeply moved." Quite literally, "he was brimming with indignation and churning inside." Was he upset at human unbelief? No, Martha said she believed. Was he angry for not arriving soon enough? No, Jesus acted on his own timetable. What was the reason for his tears? Perhaps he was indignant at the destructive forces in creation that killed Lazarus. Elsewhere in the Gospel of John, Jesus said, "I have come to bring life, and to bring it in abundance." Yet people still die. At the tomb of Lazarus, Jesus may have wept tears of indignation.

In a small town in Pennsylvania, a twenty-year-old man died tragically. He drank too much one Saturday night. While driving home, he flipped his Jeep, causing it to explode and burst into flames. The young man died. Four days later, the funeral was muted and full of quiet tears. At the side of the grave, however, his two brothers suddenly began to weep, wail, and pound on the casket. One of them shouted at the top of his lungs, "It's not right!" In the name of Jesus Christ, the giver of abundant life, the man's brother spoke the truth.

In that light, the words "Jesus wept" sound like words of resistance. They announce how wrong it is for loved ones to die prematurely. They shake an angry fist at the forces of evil and destruction, and cry out for justice and divine restoration. When Jesus wept, therefore, he stood against the ways of death. His angry tears looked like an act of holy resistance. William Billings, a noted eighteenth century musician, put it this way:

> *When Jesus wept, the falling tear*
> *In mercy flowed beyond all bound;*
> *When Jesus groaned, a trembling fear*
> *Seized all the guilty world around.*[2]

The world was put on notice when Jesus arrived in Bethany that day. He wept tears of sympathy, choosing to associate himself with those who mourn. He wept tears of indignation, affirming death as our common enemy. Yet the good news is Jesus wept tears of *action*. It was not enough for him to weep over the world's pain, or to distinguish between God's way and the ways of the world. Jesus committed himself to make a difference in the face of death. He arrived in Bethany to offer a way out of death for people who don't know any way out.

The Gospel of John says Jesus acted, but only on his terms and only according to his timetable. When he heard Lazarus was ill, Jesus didn't drop everything and rush to the bedside of his sick friend. Instead he remained where he was for two days longer. By the time he went to Bethany, Lazarus had been stone-cold in the tomb for four days. When Jesus arrived in Bethany, he seemed strangely free from gushy sentiments or emotional entanglements. He went on his own initiative, not in response to human demand or personal request. He embodied the gracious initiative of God, who moves toward us before we ask for help, who loves us before we love him, who comes to bring abundant life even when we are captive to the ways of death.

What's more, the writer of John insists Jesus already knew what he was going to do. He had known Lazarus would die. He knew God's power would be revealed by raising Lazarus from the dead. Most of all, Jesus knew the revelation of God's power would have dangerous implications. Indeed, by raising Lazarus, he set in motion the events leading up to his own death. In Jerusalem, the religious leaders were afraid of losing control. The high council huddled in fear, afraid of Roman "involvement." The high priest concluded, "It is better that the one man Jesus should die, so the rest of us will not be destroyed."

Jesus knew this, too, and he chose to undergo death for the sake of our lives. As he says elsewhere: "I am the good shepherd. The good shepherd lays down his life for the sheep. No one takes my life from me, but I lay it down of my own accord. I have power to lay it down, and I have power to take it up again. I have received this command from my Father" (John 10:11,18).

The raising of Lazarus would lead to the death of Jesus, and Jesus knew it. When Jesus wept, he faced the inevitability of his own death. This was the Gethsemane moment in the Gospel of John. By choosing to bring Lazarus out of the tomb, Jesus chose to go into his own tomb. The One who invited potential disciples to "come and see" the works of God made known in him was invited at the tomb of Lazarus to "come and see" the inevitable consequences of his life-giving works in a world of death.[3] From the beginning of time, he shared his life with the Eternal One. With tears of quiet commitment, Jesus gave the gift of his life to the world. Through the tears of his impending crucifixion we were baptized into the life of his resurrection.

The life of the Eternal One is a free gift. We participate in this eternal life by trusting Jesus, who was dead but now lives. Reflecting on the raising of Lazarus, the Episcopalian priest Robert Capon once wrote:

> **Jesus never meets a corpse that doesn't sit up right on the spot...** *They all rise not because Jesus does a number on them, not because he puts some magical resurrection machinery into gear, but simply because **he has that effect on the dead**. They rise because he is the Resurrection even before he himself rises — because, in other words, he is the grand sacrament, the real presence, of the mystery of a kingdom in which everybody rises.*[4]

Lazarus died. Jesus raised him back to life. Lazarus died again, quite possibly at the hands of those who killed Jesus.[5] And the Risen Lord raised him once again. This is the good news: in all of our deadness and death, God-in-Christ raises us up and fills us with the life of eternity. Our hope is not merely a dream of resurrection on the last day, but eternal life that begins today in faith and continues on the other side of the grave.

Such life is a gift. Receiving the gift is easy. All we need to do is trust the One who says, "I am the resurrection and the life. Those who believe in me, even though they die, will live, and everyone who believes in me will never die."

Do you believe this?

_____

1. "Tears in Heaven," Eric Clapton and Will Jennings, Unichappell Music Inc. and Blue Sky Rider Songs, 1992.

2. William Billings, "When Jesus Wept," *The Presbyterian Hymnal* (Louisville: Westminster/John Knox Press, 1990), p. 312.

3. Fred B. Craddock, *John* (Atlanta: John Knox Press, 1982), pp. 87-88.

4. Robert Farrar Capon, *The Parables of Judgment* (Grand Rapids: William B. Eerdmans Publishing Company, 1989), p. 66.

5. See John 12:9-11.

Double
Image

"You know why I want to join the church?" The speaker was a father in his thirties, holding an infant on his shoulder. A red Land's End diaper bag was slung over his other shoulder. His wife stood next to him in the church narthex, holding the hand of a cranky two-year-old with a runny nose. The father said, "We began to worry about raising our children. There are too many opinions about what's right and what's wrong, too many temptations, too many possible wrong turns. We want our kids to learn some positive values, and the church seemed like a place where they can learn them. We want to join the church because the church is one place that teaches good values."

Most young parents understand his concern. We have come through a period of about thirty years where many voices in our culture have attempted to be value-free. Child psychologists have told parents, "Don't burden your children with your moral opinions. They have to decide for themselves what is right and wrong." Therapists have invited clients to enter a judgment-free room and say whatever they wish, without fear of recourse or punishment. Even some church leaders have said, "It is not our role to tell people what to think. At best we help them clarify what is already on their minds." For the last thirty years, many people have reacted against the kind of authoritarianism that squelches freedom and denies diversity.

Yet as we approach a new century, the moral climate has changed. Pastors increasingly hear people admit that they are not sure what they believe. Life in the '90s is perplexing and ambiguous. People want guidance. They ask for direction. As one frustrated woman said to her support group, "Don't just sit there and accept me — tell me what I need to hear!" Churches in our time that offer simple answers to complex questions of right and wrong are churches that seem to grow quickly, much to the chagrin of those of us who live with complexity. Nevertheless, something must be said. A clear word is needed for confusing times.

It is good news, then, that Jesus was a teacher. According to the Gospel of Matthew, Jesus climbed a mountain like a new Moses and taught with authority unlike anybody else. In the first gospel, there are five large collections of his teachings, analogous to the five books of the Jewish law. If Jesus' teachings are the core of Matthew's book, the most important collection of his teachings is the Sermon on the Mount. And if the Sermon on the Mount is the central collection of Jesus' teachings, then the beatitudes are the heart of the Sermon on the Mount. The blessings he offers are glimpses of the kingdom he proclaims, for they point to the values which are honored within the dominion of God. Whom does God bless? The poor in spirit, those who mourn, the meek, the merciful, the peacemakers, the pure in heart, those hungry and thirsty for righteousness, and those persecuted for righteousness' sake.

Needless to say, the pronunciation of blessings on such people is an act that most of us don't completely understand. Jesus' beatitudes list a variety of characteristics that sketch the kingdom on earth as it is in heaven. Yet precisely here, where we expect his teachings to be the clearest, the full meaning of what he says lies outside our reach. As he offers a glimpse of the kingdom and its fundamental values, we stumble down the mountain somewhat dizzy and gasping for breath. We are not sure how to understand the beatitudes.

Scholars have their opinions, of course. Some interpreters of Matthew say the beatitudes offer *a glimpse of the future*, a peek of the day when every tear shall be dried and suffering shall be no more. Regardless of whatever distress we experience today, the beatitudes announce that someday God will set things right. After all, Jesus says those who mourn will be comforted. Those who hunger and thirst for righteousness will be satisfied. The beatitudes give us hope for the future. They keep us going in the present by pointing to what lies ahead.

On the morning before Bill Clinton took the presidential oath of office, he went to a nearby church for a prayer service. Someone read the beatitudes during the service. When the reader came to the last two verses, someone observed Mr. Clinton mouthing the words of Jesus: "Blessed are you when people revile you and persecute you and utter all kinds of evil against you falsely on my account. Rejoice and be glad, for your reward is great in heaven."[1] They were good words for a politician to say, particularly on the opening day of what turned out to be a rocky term of office. Any American politician who tries to take an occasional stand for what is holy, just, and true can expect persecution, slander, and false accounts. The only reward may be a heavenly one.

Some scholars claim we should interpret the beatitudes in terms of their promised final reward. "If you are mourning now, someday you will be comforted." "If you are hungry for justice today, in the future you will be satisfied."

The problem with this interpretation, however, is that Jesus doesn't keep his tenses straight. He mixes present tense with the future tense. "Blessed *are* the meek," he says in the present tense, "for they *shall* inherit the earth," in the future tense. "Blessed *are* the poor in spirit, for theirs *is* the kingdom of heaven," here and now in the present. Is he speaking of now or then? We can't be sure.

Other interpreters say this mixture of future and present indicates the purpose behind these teachings. The beatitudes point us toward God's future, to be sure, but this future is already mixed like leaven in the dough of present-day life. That is, the beatitudes offer not merely a glimpse of God's future, but a vision of how we can live today.

All things considered, that, too, is a good interpretation. You may have noticed that Jesus does not address the beatitudes to anybody in particular. As he teaches on the mountain, he releases his blessings into the air. "Blessed are the meek," whoever they are. "Blessed are the merciful," wherever they may be. "Blessed are the peacemakers," whoever, wherever. If the blessing fits our circumstances, welcome to the kingdom! If it doesn't fit, we can put ourselves in a position to receive the blessing. If we desire a happy life, we must get out into the world and be poor in spirit. If we want to be blessed, we must become peacemakers.

This is a good interpretation of the beatitudes. The problem is it doesn't work like a scientific formula. There is no assurance that anybody who tries to live out the beatitudes will turn out to be happy or blessed.

In the last century, a Belgian priest named Father Damien went to live on a remote island colony among people with leprosy. Father Damien tried to live the values of the beatitudes. He was pure in heart, merciful, hungry and thirsty for righteousness. He was publicly persecuted for doing what he believed was right. His biographers also say he was often lonely, depressed, and stubborn. His immediate superiors branded him a troublemaker.[2] Despite failed attempts within the Roman Catholic church to name him as a saint, few people who knew Father Damien called him "happy" or "blessed."

There is no simple assurance that living the beatitudes will make somebody's life a blessed bed of roses. We can claim them as values to teach our children and virtues to pursue in daily life, but they are not stepping stones for success, at least not in this age. As someone said, "Blessed are the meek? Try being meek tomorrow when you go to work and see how far you get. Meekness is fine for church, but in the *real* world, the meek get to go home early with a pink slip and a pat on the back."[3]

It is difficult to understand the beatitudes of Jesus. Perhaps this wild, untamed quality is the very source of their power.[4] Anybody who learns these words from the Gospel of Matthew may not understand them right away. Whoever takes these teachings seriously may wonder how Jesus can actually say them in such a rough and aggressive world. They do not comfort anxious parents, give quick assurances to politicians, or promise relief for feisty priests. But they do unsettle us. If these blessings by Jesus are truly inscribed upon our hearts, they prompt us to wonder whether or not they are true. Are the poor in spirit blessed by God? Is God revealed to the pure in heart? Will God give the earth as a free inheritance to the meek? We cannot know completely unless we are following Jesus, who epitomized what it means to be meek, pure, and poor in spirit. Does God show mercy to the merciful? Does God claim those who are persecuted for the sake of righteousness? We cannot be sure until we have been set free by the death and resurrection of Jesus, who claims us in mercy. When we are sufficiently unsettled by the living word of the living Christ, then the beatitudes can offer their blessing.

A bricklayer from Texas died a few years ago. Many Texans freely admit they are not generally known for their meekness or gentleness. As someone notes, they are a flinty people formed by a dry wind that blows across a hard land. A true Texan is typically full of bluster, not humility. Yet this bricklayer was a follower of Jesus Christ, and his discipleship tempered him into a gentle man. It was most evident in his work.

At the memorial service, his son offered an eloquent testimony of how the father's faith had affected the quality of his daily work. If customers wanted quick and cheap work, this man took his time to do the job well and asked for a fair wage. When inferior brick became available, he refused to take shortcuts in his building materials. He never made a lot of money or received widespread fame, yet he rested in the confidence of a hard day's work done well.

What kind of life does God value? We cannot really know until we follow Jesus Christ to the point that it makes a difference in how we live. God's blessing comes not to those who pursue meekness, but to those who pursue Jesus Christ and welcome God's earth as a holy inheritance. Satisfaction comes not to those who work to make themselves righteous, but to those hungry for *God's* righteousness, as revealed in the cross of Jesus.

The beatitudes of Jesus announce a realm of values that press us to ask where we belong. Do we belong to a world of persecution, war-making, and death? Or do we belong to a realm of mercy and comfort, purity and righteousness? Daily life can confuse us, until we claim our place among Christ's unfinished saints. As we follow Jesus, the blessing of the Gospel is that we begin to see the realm of God which this world does not yet see.

Frederick Buechner tells about watching a scene in the Ken Burns film series on the Civil War. It was the fiftieth anniversary of the Battle of Gettysburg, and veterans from North and South gathered at the battleground to reminisce. At one point, the veterans decided to reenact Pickett's Charge. All the participants took their positions, and then one side began to charge the other. Instead of swords and rifles, this time the vets carried canes and crutches. As both sides converged, the old men did not fight. Instead they embraced and began to weep.

Buechner muses, "If only those doddering old veterans had seen in 1863 what they now saw so clearly fifty years later." Then he adds:

> *Half a century later, they saw that the great battle had been a great madness. The men who were advancing toward them across the field of Gettysburg were not enemies. They were human beings like themselves, with the same dreams, needs, hopes, the same wives and children waiting for them to come home . . . What they saw was that we were, all of us, created not to do battle with each other but to love each other, and it was not just a truth they saw. For a few minutes, it was a truth they lived. It was a truth they became.*[5]

Where do we belong? When we look out the window, we see a world of division and war. There are debts to pay and dangers that scare us to death. It looks like our children are at risk, and the future seems tenuous.

But now and then, as we follow Jesus, this weary, old world is unmasked as an illusion, and we see beyond a shadow of a doubt that the kingdom of heaven is at hand.

1. As reported by Michael McManus, *Scranton Times* 24 January 1993.

2. Gavan Daws, *Holy Man* (Honolulu: University of Hawaii Press, 1984), p. 249.

3. William H. Willimon, *On a Wild and Windy Mountain* (Nashville: Abingdon Press, 1984), p, 66.

4. I am indebted to Thomas G. Long for this insight, which comes from a sermon he preached to The Homiletical Feast, Princeton, NJ, 18 January 1993.

5. Frederick Buechner, "Journey Toward Wholeness," *Theology Today* 49/4 (January 1993), pp. 454-464.

Between
The Parentheses

Whenever a preacher announces a sermon text from the book of Revelation, a lot of people grow nervous. Revelation is widely regarded as the most confusing book in the Bible. The book is chock-full of strange visions, eerie sounds, and jolting images. Wild-eyed interpreters have offered curious interpretations of the future, turning to Revelation and neglecting the rest of the Bible. In short, the book of Revelation has been considered a happy hunting ground for heretics. It is no wonder that many Christians are afraid of their own book.

Even so, the book of Revelation may also be one of our great undiscovered treasures. It was first addressed as a letter to the church during uncertain and dangerous times. The original name of the book is the "Apocalypse," which means a disclosure. In the Bible, an apocalypse is a moment when God pulls back the curtain that hides heaven from earth. The Revelation offers glimpses of a holy reality which is normally hid from our eyes.

Today we hear a voice from heaven announcing, "I am the Alpha and the Omega." That unusual expression appears three times in the final book of the Bible. Each time the voice speaks, we learn something about God that is crucial to our faith and life.

The first insight has to do with a simple observation about language. When God says, "I am the Alpha and Omega," alumni/ae of college fraternities may sit up straight in their pews, for they hear God equating himself with two letters from the Greek alphabet. In a Bible full of words, God announces he is made known through the letters from human alphabets. These letters combine into words. Words are spoken. God's speech makes a world. That is how it was in the beginning, and how it shall be in God's new creation. The primary tools used by the Creator of heaven and earth are words. Whenever God speaks, something happens.

In one of his autobiographical reflections, Frederick Buechner reflects on the power of God to create each new day. It is a creative, holy force expressed through words. As he writes:

> *Darkness was upon the face of the deep, and God said, "Let there be light." Darkness laps at my sleeping face like a tide, and God says, "Let there be Buechner." Why not? Out of the primeval chaos of sleep (God) calls me to be a life again...To wake up is to be given back your life again. To wake up is to be given back the world again and of all possible worlds this world...Waking into the new day, we are all of us Adam on the morning of creation, and the world is ours to name. Out of many fragments we are called to put back together a self again.*[1]

Every morning, the word that puts us back together is the same word that spoke the world into being. If God has been around since the first day of creation, God has seen it all, heard it all, and spoken it all. Certainly God does not speak any new words that he has not spoken before. In fact, when God declares, "I am the Alpha and the Omega," the words echo a passage from the prophet Isaiah's poetry where God says, "I am the first and the last" (Isaiah 44:6).

As scholars point out, there is no new word spoken in the book of Revelation. Of the 404 verses of this book, there are 518 allusions to earlier passages of scripture.[2] The writer of this book points to the books of Exodus, Daniel, Zechariah, and the Psalms, among others. John does not simply string together words from other books, so much as he points to the one Word in which all other words are held together. Ever since Genesis, God has spoken a lot of words. By the time we arrive at the book of Revelation, only one Word captures all God has to say, and that is the Word made flesh, Jesus Christ. John points us to Jesus as the central Word in the vocabulary of faith.

This insight offers a constant reminder to the church about the integrating center of all we proclaim. In a certain church, the pastor stood at the door after worship one Sunday, waiting for compliments on the weekly homiletical masterpiece. The response did not come as expected. In desperation, the preacher turned to a wise friend from the congregation and asked, "How did I do this morning?" The friend shrugged the shoulders and mumbled a few pleasantries. These words also did not satisfy, so the preacher said, "No, really, I want to know what you thought of what I said in my sermon today."

"Sorry," said the friend, "I wasn't listening to you; I was too busy paying attention to Jesus."

Now, that is good preaching. Behind every preacher, prayer, or scripture passage, the wise person listens for the Word beyond all human words. Jesus Christ is "the one Word of God which we have to hear and which we have to trust and obey in life and in death."[3] When God reveals himself as the Alpha and the Omega, he tells us first and foremost that he draws near through words which point to Jesus Christ.

Yet something more can be said. Alpha and Omega are more than mere letters in the alphabet; they are the first and last letters. In fact, no sooner does God say, "I am the Alpha and the Omega," than a voice in a vision goes on to say, "I am the first and the last" (Revelation 1:17, 22:13). God alone speaks the first and last words on human life. No other person, power, or principality can say what God alone can say.

In April 1995, there was a baptism in the Russian city of Ananuri. With little fanfare or advance notice, Pavel Grachev, the Russian defense minister, walked into an Orthodox church and asked to be baptized. "It took place quite unexpectedly," noted a church official. Grachev was a commander of Soviet occupation forces in Afghanistan for five years. During the war in Chechnya, he was widely criticized for his army's brutality. He went to Ananuri to sign an agreement on the shared use of military bases. By the end of that week, Grachev had been baptized.[4]

By all appearances, Grachev was a soldier in search of a war. But now he has been claimed in the strong name of the Trinity through water and the Word. Who knows what will happen next? Now that he has been baptized, there may be a day when the Russian defense minister stands up to say, "I have decided wars, weapons, and armies are a bad idea. Once we thought they were necessary, but now they are obsolete. So I call upon all nations of the world to join me in beating our swords into plowshares."

That may sound naive. "After all," critics say, "it was only a baptism, some water splashed on a soldier's brow." But what if God is good for his promises? What if God begins to intrude upon Grachev's career and moves us closer to the final day of peace? What if God has the first word and last laugh on Grachev's life?

"I am the Alpha and the Omega, the first and the last" (Revelation 22:13). The faithful church lives in this promise. While Revelation is full of unsettling visions and disturbing pictures, the first word of this book is identical to the last word. The beginning and the end are the same. As the writer addresses this book to the church, he greets them by saying, "Grace to you, and peace from him who is, and who was, and who is to come" (Revelation 1:4). As the book comes to an end, the last words are, "The grace of the Lord Jesus be with all the saints." In between there is much in this book that unsettles a sensitive stomach. But the first word and the last word are the same . . . and the word is *grace*. It is a word that God alone can say.

Like all the words God speaks, grace is a word that makes sense only when we look to Jesus Christ. Through Christ, God is relentlessly inclined in our favor. According to our text, Jesus is the "faithful witness" who points to the truth of God's love. He is "the firstborn of the dead," who has opened the way of resurrection. Jesus is ruler over the earth's royalty, exalted as King of kings and Lord of lords. He is "the One who loves us," and "the One who sets us free by his blood." He makes us to be a kingdom of priests. He is coming so that every eye will see him.

The work of grace is not finished yet. Sometimes our world seems enchanted with its own destruction. Yet for a few moments this morning the curtain is drawn back and we catch a glimpse of how God pursues us through the love of Jesus Christ. Thanks to such grace, we belong to a God who has set us free and will never let us go.

Yet one thing more must be said. God says, "I am the Alpha and the Omega," and promises to speak to us the ancient word that makes all things new. God alone speaks the first and last word on human existence, which is a surprisingly gracious word. The third time God says, "I am the Alpha and the Omega," he affirms, "I am the beginning and the end" (Revelation 22:13, 21:6). Perhaps this is our greatest hope: that God will be both our source and our destination. Through the grace of Christ our king, we trust that the God who gave us birth will complete and finish our lives.

Daily problems can blur our vision. When caught up in neighborhood scandals or shady deals, we may forget the One who made us. When a day care center blows up in Oklahoma City, we think, "What's this world coming to?" Listen: every day is full of enough hassles and horrors to shake up the strongest soul. Each one of us needs a place to stand and a promise to cling to.

Some days all we can do is hang on by our fingernails, and trust the One "who is, who was, who is to come." We hope for God, and remember God. We remember God's saving history and hope for God's final victory. As one of the great hymns of the church has expressed the essence of faith,

> *Through many dangers, toils, and snares,*
> *I have already come;*
> *'Tis grace has led me safe thus far,*
> *and grace will lead me home.*[5]

The late New Testament scholar Joachim Jeremias grew up as a child of German missionaries in Israel. When the Third Reich came to power, the relationship between the German people and the Jewish people became hostile and painful. The family left. Then came the second world war and the Holocaust. Years later, Jeremias wished to return to Israel. He wanted to see if anybody remembered him as a young person, and would say to him, "Joachim, we forgive you."

He said, "I returned to Israel long after the war. I knocked on door after door. I couldn't find anybody. I came to one house and thought surely someone is here, and they will let me in. I knocked and a man answered. I remembered him. "I'm Joachim Jeremias." The man said, "Please come in.""

"It is good you came at this time," said the Jewish host. "We are celebrating the feast of Succoth, which is the festival of tabernacles. Come into our back yard."

The family had erected a booth for the feast. There was a brush arbor, with fruit hanging down. The family would enter through a little doorway and tell the story of Israel's life in the wilderness. Professor Jeremias noticed a little piece of paper clipped to one side of the doorway, and another piece of paper clipped to the other side of the doorway. There was a word on one side and another word on the other side. The words were in Hebrew. Jeremias asked his host, "What are those words?"

He replied, "That is a summary of Psalm 139: 'Where can I go from your spirit? Or where can I flee from your presence? If I ascend to heaven, you are there; if I make my bed in Sheol, you are there. If I take the wings of the morning and settle at the farthest limits of the sea, even there your hand shall lead me, and your right hand shall hold me fast'" (Psalm 139:7-10).

Jeremias said, "I don't understand." The man said, "Well, that word on the left is 'from God.' This word on the right is 'to God.' In between, we live from God . . . to God."[6]

Those are the parentheses around my life and your life. We live "from God to God." Our final destination is to arrive at the Source of our life. The aim of every life is to return to the God from whom all things were made, and in whose purposes all creation shall be completed. In between new creation and final consummation, we have a place to stand and a promise to claim. We belong to God, the Alpha and the Omega, the first and the last, the beginning and the end. And as poet T. S. Eliot once wrote:

> ... *the end of all our exploring*
> *Will be to arrive where we started*
> *And know the place for the first time.*[7]

1. Frederick Buechner, *The Alphabet of Grace* (New York: The Seabury Press, 1970), pp. 21-22.

2. Eugene H. Peterson, *Reversed Thunder: The Revelation of John and the Praying Imagination* (San Francisco: Harper & Row, 1988), pp. 22-23.

3. "Theological Declaration of Barmen," *The Book of Confessions* (Louisville: Presbyterian Church USA, 1991) 8.11.

4. "Russian Defense Minister Baptized," *Ecumenical News International* 18 April 1995.

5. *Presbyterian Hymnal* (Louisville: Westminster/John Knox Press, 1990), p. 280.

6. I am grateful to Fred B. Craddock for this story.

7. T. S. Eliot, "Little Gidding," *Four Quartets* (New York: Harcourt, Brace, 1943), p. 59.

It Is Blessed
To Receive

In the small town of Mapleville, the ecumenical Thanksgiving Eve service was poorly attended. Once it was a popular event for the whole town, gathering people from a variety of denominations and faiths. In recent years, attendance had faded to a faithful few. Most of those who came in any given year were members of the host congregation. What began as a spirited occasion that brought together a variety of clergy, choirs, and congregations had shrunk in numbers and dwindled in enthusiasm.

One minister was particularly frustrated by the meager turnout. When the Mapleville clergy association asked him to preach one year, he nailed together a sermon on the story of Jesus and the ten lepers. Climbing into the pulpit, he retold the story of how the ten approached Jesus and begged for mercy. The Lord commanded them to show themselves to the priests. On their way in obedience, the lepers were made clean. Only one of them turned around, returned to Jesus, and offered thanks.

"As I look out over this sparse congregation," the preacher said, "I ask myself: where are the nine? Why aren't they here, giving thanks? Aren't they grateful enough to come to church?"

One by one, folks in the congregation began to nod their heads in smug recognition. They smiled as the minister said, "Think of all those people who will sit before a fat table of turkey and stuffing, yet who did not come tonight to thank the founder of their feast." One by one, the people began to glow with satisfaction as the minister said, "Nine lepers ignored the One who gave them the gift of healing. Yet one was grateful enough to say thanks."

Unfortunately, it never occurred to anybody present how they were being compared to a leper who was also a hated Samaritan. What's more, nobody (including the preacher) realized the deep irony of how much of that year's Thanksgiving service was spent chastising those who were not thankful, and how little energy was spent in generating genuine gratitude.[1]

The story of Jesus and the ten lepers recognizes gratitude as a theological problem. Thankfulness comes and goes like every other human emotion. There's no telling why the tenth leper turned back in gratitude while the others did not. He had every reason to press on to see the priests, for that would hasten his return to society and his reunion with loved ones.[2]

Why did he turn back? Luke says the man was singing from the top of his lungs; maybe the other nine wanted some peace and quiet, and asked him to leave. Since all ten lepers were healed, perhaps the ugly divisions returned between Jews and Samaritans when they were no longer bound together by a common illness. Perhaps, as a foreigner, the tenth leper discovered on the road he did not have a priest like the others. Where else could he go, but back to Jesus? Whatever the reason, the text offers no explanation why he returned to offer thanks and others did not. While nine former companions moved ahead to claim their future, he paused, turned back, and said, "Thank you!" There is no obvious reason for his return. No one prompted him to do it. Neither did anyone urge him to say thanks. All we know is *this man, more than anybody else, knew how to receive a gift.*

Is there any trait more admirable or any virtue more noble than this? It is a rare person who can regularly open grateful hands to receive a gift. Sometimes it takes an entire lifetime to learn how to do it well.

A man had mixed memories of Christmas. As a child, he began planning for the holiday in February. He scribbled out a wish list for the following December 25 before the winter snow melted off the ground. Each year he listed a full page of toys which he wanted more than anything else. Then he waited impatiently for Christmas. His annual anticipation was tempered by the presence of his mother, who insisted on thank-you notes for every gift received.

> *Every present under our Christmas tree was just the visible tip of an iceberg of obligation. My mother tracked each package as meticulously as a U.P.S. driver, and her master list haunted my siblings and me for the rest of winter vacation. Bells would be ringing, snow would be falling, our friends would be sliding down our street on brand-new Flexible Flyers — and my sister, my brother, and I would be bent over tear-spattered sheets of stationery, whimpering.*[3]

There is no assurance that a gift received will prompt the person who receives it to say, "Thank you." Sometimes a parent hovers over a child to enforce gratitude, thus killing it. Other times, gifts are given with strings attached, making it virtually impossible for the recipient to offer thanks.

In *Spoon River Anthology*, Edgar Lee Masters reports the epitaphs of the people of Spoon River, Illinois. From the grave, the townspeople tell the truth about their lives. One woman, Constance Hately, reveals why two adopted nieces grew up to despise her.

> *You praise my self-sacrifice, Spoon River,*
> *In rearing Irene and Mary,*
> *Orphans of my older sister!*
> *And you censure Irene and Mary*
> *For their contempt for me!*
> *But praise not my self-sacrifice,*
> *And censure not their contempt;*
> *I reared them, I cared for them, true enough! —*
> *But I poisoned my benefactions*
> *With constant reminders of their dependence.*[4]

All through their lives, under the guise of generosity, Constance said, "Girls, I took you in when your mother died, and I never want you to forget it." As long as they lived beneath her roof, as long as they sat at her table, they were reminded how their very lives depended on their long-suffering aunt. In time, they grew to detest her.

There may be no moment more beautiful or damaging than the giving of a gift. How we handle such a moment will reveal what we are made of. More than that, it will reveal what God is doing within our hearts. In the New Testament, the occasion is so profound that the same word is used for both the giving and the receiving of the gift. The word is *charis*, which is translated "grace." As one scholar has written, "The word may refer to a favor shown or a favor received. (It) may define an act of giving or an act of receiving: if giving, the word means 'gift or unearned favor'; if receiving, then the word is best translated 'gratitude.' Since the same term represents both sides of the act, it is natural to expect that grace as gift would be met with grace as gratitude."[5]

Gratitude is a genuine miracle of God. Like the apostle Paul, most of us would ascribe to Jesus the saying, "It is more blessed to give than to receive" (Acts 20:35).[6] Good Christian people have often given themselves to selfless charity, and remained reticent to welcome any gift. As a result, churches are full of people who are experts at giving. They spend hours with needy children. They volunteer to serve on a hundred different committees. They sign up for payroll deductions for United Way. They stay awake until 2:00 a.m. to listen to somebody with a broken heart. They always have time for everybody and everything. They give constantly. Yet if you observe such people in a rare quiet moment, you may notice they know a lot about giving, and practically nothing about receiving.

Why is it so difficult to receive? I don't know. But when it comes to the Christian faith, we cannot fully believe unless we know how to receive.

The Geneva Catechism asked the question, "Should we not be grateful to other people when they perform some service for us?" The answer: "Of course we should, precisely because God honors them by channelling through their hands the good things that flow to us from the inexhaustible fountain of his generosity. In this way he puts us in their debt, and he wants us to acknowledge it. Anyone, therefore, who does not show gratitude to other people betrays ingratitude to God as well."[7]

One goal for the entire Christian life is to affirm God's generous dealings with people like us. It begins by understanding the Bible as a story of how God has given gifts to his people.

When God's children were slaves in Egypt, God brought them out of slavery with an outstretched arm and a mighty hand. God said, "You're free! It's a gift."

When God's children stumbled in their freedom and did not know how to live their lives, God gave them the Law as a lamp for their feet and a light for their path. It was a gift.

When God's children grew worn-down, burned-out, and exhausted, God said, "You can't keep going without a break. There are limits. Take a day to relax and meditate. One day in seven you shall clear the calendar to the glory of God. It's a gift."

When God's children tired of wandering in the wilderness, they needed a place to put down roots. So God said, "When you cross the river Jordan, you're going to come to a land of milk and honey. It's all yours. It's a gift." When the people needed rulers, God gave them judges and then kings. When the people needed a place to worship, God gave them a temple. When the people needed forgiveness, God gave them a day of atonement. When the people forgot everything God had done for them, God gave them prophets.

Then, one day, God gave them Jesus Christ, who in turn gave his very life as a gift.

We cannot understand the Bible unless we know what it means to receive. We cannot know the faith of the church until we know how to open our hands in gratitude. It is the very nature of God to give generously, even "to the ungrateful and the wicked" (Luke 6:35). Blessed is the one who can say, "Thank you."

We have heard it said, "It is more blessed to give than to receive." But today we also affirm, "It is blessed to receive." Every one of us has received something. We don't have anything to give, except as we have received. Every breath of life, every heartbeat, every conscious thought is a gift. Every person we meet, every friend we make, every relationship that warms the heart and challenges the soul is a gift. Every opportunity to work, every meaningful task, every dollar earned is a gift. Our lifelong task is learning how to receive the gifts of God with gratitude and graciousness.

During summer vacations from seminary, I worked for a county highway department. While other students worked for the kingdom as summer camp leaders and youth group interns, I filled potholes and scooped up roadkill. A graduate school degree was unimportant to my supervisors, so I quickly found myself at the bottom of the pecking order doing tasks no one else would do. The only person lower than me was a man in his sixties named Elvin. By most standards, his life was pathetic. He never got beyond the third grade. His wife ran off with another man. His daughter was a teenage runaway. Elvin couldn't read or write. He was the butt of all the jokes at the highway department.

He was a tragic human being, except in one regard. Every day Elvin opened his lunch box and pulled out a bologna sandwich. Shutting his eyes, he prayed, "I thank you, O Lord, for this good bounty from your good earth." Elvin didn't have much to make him grateful. He had a meager job and some co-workers who constantly poked fun behind his back. He had a set of work clothes, a place to sleep, and an old crusty sandwich. It wasn't very much. But every noon, he spoke a few fragile words revealing a heart full of gratitude.

We have a God who is generous in all seasons, giving us gifts that we do not expect, inclining toward us with a grace we do not deserve. God keeps giving, for it is God's very nature to give. And the final work of God is not merely to fill our lives with good things, but to teach us to receive them with thanks. The road to gratitude is a lifelong journey, but as far as I'm concerned it is the only trip worth taking.

The place to begin is with a prayer once written by the poet George Herbert. He prayed, "Thou that hast given so much to me, Give one thing more: a grateful heart."[8]

---

1. The idea for this story comes from Fred B. Craddock, in "Preaching About Giving Thanks: Giving God Thanks and Praise," *Preaching In and Out of Season*, Thomas G. Long and Neely Dixon McCarter, editors (Louisville: Westminster/John Knox Press, 1990), p. 120.

2. See Leviticus 13 and 14 for a description of the process by which lepers were restored to community life.

3. David Owen, "No Thanks," *The New Yorker* 18 December 1995: p. 128.

4. Edgar Lee Masters, *Spoon River Anthology* (New York: Signet Classic, 1992), p. 10.

5. Craddock, 121.

6. Curiously, this saying does not appear in the four gospels, causing some scholars to doubt its authenticity.

7. As quoted by B. A. Gerrish, *Grace and Gratitude: The Eucharistic Theology of John Calvin* (Minneapolis: Fortress Press, 1993), p. 45.

8. George Herbert, "Gratefulnesse," *The English Poems of George Herbert* (Totowa, NJ: Dent, Rowman, and Littlefield, 1978), pp. 135-6.

Lectionary Preaching
After Pentecost

Virtually all pastors who make use of the sermons in this book will find their worship life and planning shaped by one of two lectionary series. Most mainline Protestant denominations, along with clergy of the Roman Catholic Church, have now approved — either for provisional or official use — the three-year Revised Common (Consensus) Lectionary. This family of denominations includes United Methodist, Presbyterian, United Church of Christ and Disciples of Christ. Recently the ELCA division of Lutheranism also began following the Revised Common Lectionary. This change has been reflected in the headings and scripture listings with each sermon in this book.

Roman Catholics and Lutheran divisions other than ELCA follow their own three-year cycle of texts. While there are divergences between the Revised Common and Roman Catholic/Lutheran systems, the gospel texts show striking parallels, with few text selections evidencing significant differences. Nearly all the gospel texts included in this book will, therefore, be applicable to worship and preaching planning for clergy following either lectionary.

A significant divergence does occur, however, in the method by which specific gospel texts assigned to specific calendar days. The Revised Common and Roman Catholic Lectionaries accomplish this by counting backwards from Christ the King (Last Sunday after Pentecost), discarding "extra" texts from the front of the list: Lutherans (not using the Revised Common Lectionary) follow the opposite pattern, counting forward from The Holy Trinity, discarding "extra" texts at the end of the list.

The following index will aid the user of this book in matching the correct text to the correct Sunday during the Pentecost portion of the church year.

(Fixed dates do not pertain to Lutheran Lectionary)

Fixed Date Lectionaries *Revised Common (including ELCA)* *and Roman Catholic*	Lutheran Lectionary *Lutheran*
The Day of Pentecost	The Day of Pentecost
The Holy Trinity	The Holy Trinity
May 29-June 4 — Proper 4, Ordinary Time 9	Pentecost 2
June 5-11 — Proper 5, Ordinary Time 10	Pentecost 3
June 12-18 — Proper 6, Ordinary Time 11	Pentecost 4

June 19-25 — Proper 7, Ordinary Time 12	Pentecost 5
June 26-July 2 — Proper 8, Ordinary Time 13	Pentecost 6
July 3-9 — Proper 9, Ordinary Time 14	Pentecost 7
July 10-16 — Proper 10, Ordinary Time 15	Pentecost 8
July 17-23 — Proper 11, Ordinary Time 16	Pentecost 9
July 24-30 — Proper 12, Ordinary Time 17	Pentecost 10
July 31-Aug. 6 — Proper 13, Ordinary Time 18	Pentecost 11
Aug. 7-13 — Proper 14, Ordinary Time 19	Pentecost 12
Aug. 14-20 — Proper 15, Ordinary Time 20	Pentecost 13
Aug. 21-27 — Proper 16, Ordinary Time 21	Pentecost 14
Aug. 28-Sept. 3 — Proper 17, Ordinary Time 22	Pentecost 15
Sept. 4-10 — Proper 18, Ordinary Time 23	Pentecost 16
Sept. 11-17 — Proper 19, Ordinary Time 24	Pentecost 17
Sept. 18-24 — Proper 20, Ordinary Time 25	Pentecost 18
Sept. 25-Oct. 1 — Proper 21, Ordinary Time 26	Pentecost 19
Oct. 2-8 — Proper 22, Ordinary Time 27	Pentecost 20
Oct. 9-15 — Proper 23, Ordinary Time 28	Pentecost 21
Oct. 16-22 — Proper 24, Ordinary Time 29	Pentecost 22
Oct. 23-29 — Proper 25, Ordinary Time 30	Pentecost 23
Oct. 30-Nov. 5 — Proper 26, Ordinary Time 31	Pentecost 24
Nov. 6-12 — Proper 27, Ordinary Time 32	Pentecost 25
Nov. 13-19 — Proper 28, Ordinary Time 33	Pentecost 26
	Pentecost 27
Nov. 20-26 — Christ the King	Christ the King

Reformation Day (or last Sunday in October) is October 31 (Revised Common, Lutheran)

All Saints' Day (or first Sunday in November) is November 1 (Revised Common, Lutheran, Roman Catholic)

Books In This Cycle B Series

Gospel Set
God's Downward Mobility
Sermons For Advent, Christmas And Epiphany
John A. Stroman

Which Way To Jesus?
Sermons For Lent And Easter
Harry N. Huxhold

Water Won't Quench The Fire
Sermons For Pentecost (First Third)
William G. Carter

Fringe, Front And Center
Sermons For Pentecost (Middle Third)
George W. Hoyer

No Box Seats In The Kingdom
Sermons For Pentecost (Last Third)
William G. Carter

First Lesson Set
Light In The Land Of Shadows
Sermons For Advent, Christmas And Epiphany
Harold C. Warlick, Jr.

Times Of Refreshing
Sermons For Lent and Easter
E. Carver McGriff

Lyrics For The Centuries
Sermons For Pentecost (First Third)
Arthur H. Kolsti

No Particular Place To Go
Sermons For Pentecost (Middle Third)
Timothy J. Smith

When Trouble Comes!
Sermons For Pentecost (Last Third)
Zan W. Holmes, Jr.